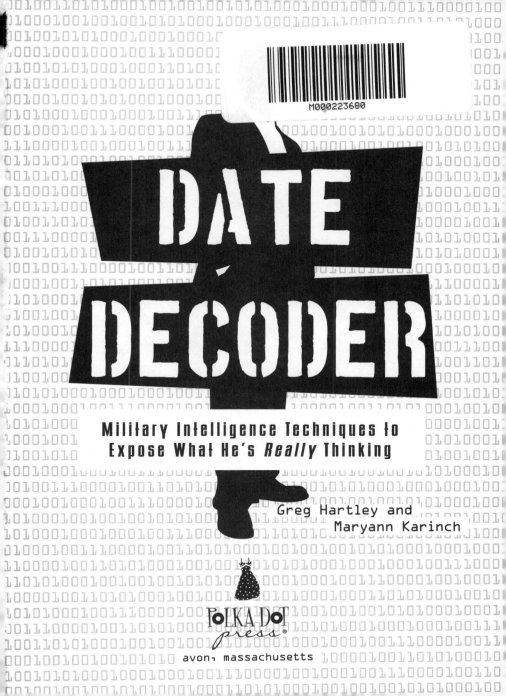

DATE DECODER

Military Intelligence Techniques to Expose What He's *Really* Thinking

Greg Hartley and
Maryann Karinch

POLKA DOT
press

avon, massachusetts

The Polka Dot Press® name and logo design are registered trademarks of
F+W Publications, Inc.

Published by Adams Media, an F+W Publications Company
57 Littlefield Street
Avon, MA 02322
www.adamsmedia.com

ISBN-13: 978-1-59869-421-5
ISBN-10: 1-59869-421-9

Library of Congress Cataloging-in-Publication Data
is available from the publisher

Printed in Canada.

J I H G F E D C B A

This publication is designed to provide accurate and authoritative information with regard to the subject matter covered. It is sold with the understanding that the publisher is not engaged in rendering legal, accounting, or other
professional advice. If legal advice or other expert assistance is required, the
services of a competent professional person should be sought.
—From a *Declaration of Principles* jointly adopted by a Committee of the
American Bar Association and a Committee of Publishers and Associations

The authors wish to note that the approaches and techniques in this book
come from the world of professional interrogation and are used as a reference only. Unqualified people should never attempt to interrogate anyone.

Many of the designations used by manufacturers and sellers to distinguish
their products are claimed as trademarks. Where those designations appear
in this book and Adams Media was aware of a trademark claim, the designations have been printed with initial capital letters.

Interior illustrations by Grant Hanna.

This book is available at quantity discounts for bulk purchases.
For information, please call 1-800-289-0963.

To Dina, my last date.

-Greg

To Jim, my favorite date. Tough to decode, but well worth the effort.

-Maryann

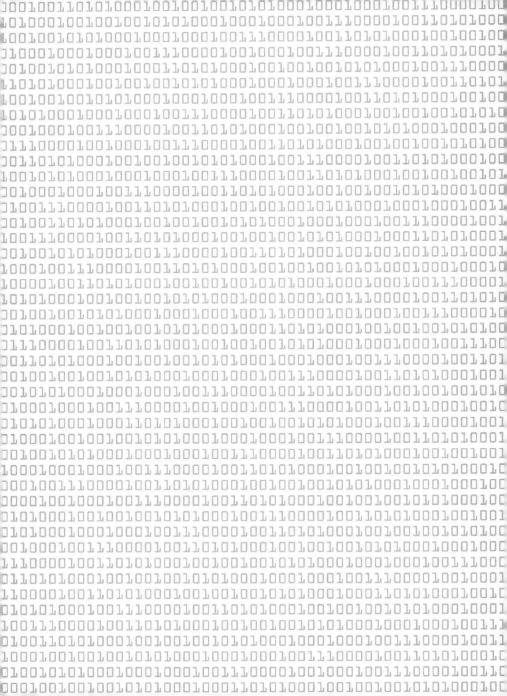

Contents

Acknowledgments

Thank you first of all to Jim McCormick, who always provides practical support and inspiration as I write all day and night. Thanks to my mom, dad, and brother for being the voices in my head that helped me make good choices. Thanks also to the wonderful men in my life (good times don't have to last forever) and even more so to the amazing girlfriends who helped me survive and thrive when the not-so-wonderful men hung around.

I want to acknowledge the enthusiastic and smart team at Adams Media that has made this project a great success: Jennifer Kushnier, Meredith O'Hayre, Virginia Beck, Stephanie Chrusz, and Colleen Cunningham. Thanks also to the many women who contributed their thoughts to Greg and me about what they look for in a man. I never realized how many women of all ages love a man who can dance.

More thanks to a few friends who gave practical input throughout the project: Patti Mengers, David Kozinski, David Kelly, Karen Pedone, and Judith Bailey.

Finally, to Cupid: If you weren't so careless, this book wouldn't be necessary.

—*Maryann Karinch*

Introduction

uick: Do the following describe dating or interrogation? Role playing, interpreting body language, manipulating emotions, and determining values. If you said *both,* you're right. The manufactured nature of the encounter is one clear thing that dating has in common with interrogation.

When I was a young soldier, I'd go to bars with my friends, set my sights on a woman, and connect with her, at least for a few hours. My buddies would say, "You big, squinty-eyed, redheaded goon! How'd you do that?" Much of it was instinct, but after I learned more about body language and psychology, I could put words to it.

Later, after years of teaching interrogation skills to U.S. intelligence and counter-intelligence personnel, one of my male students showed me a copy of Neil Strauss's *The Game* and asked if I'd read it. "Why?" I asked him. "We're interrogators. We have the tools to influence the behavior of any woman we want."

And then I realized that was *not* true. I wouldn't win over a woman who knew what I knew—unless she *chose* to be with me. Furthermore, a woman with interrogator skills is more adept at manipulating human behavior than a man (generally true of female interrogators). I'll explore the reasons for this in the book.

Interrogation is nothing more than sharpening your interpersonal skills to a razor's edge. Learning to see strength and weakness, motivating a person to do what you want him to do, and detecting deception—these are skills we all need in daily life. But these skills are never more important than when trying to choose a mate.

So this book is for any woman in the dating scene who is not a trained interrogator. This book is for any woman who doesn't want to waste her time with controlling or shallow men. Maryann and I designed this book as an interactive, practical handbook that steps you through a series of exercises that help you build interrogator-like skills while you have fun. Regardless of where you are in a relationship, whether still looking or half of a serious couple, each chapter will give you tools that I have used in the interrogation process in a way that you can use them in your dating life.

It's important you know that I'm good at what I do because of who I am as much as what I know. Throughout this book, I will tell you candid stories of my successes and failures so that you can see how I've grown.

You can choose whom you fall for, and when, and short-circuit the routines. Interrogation as I've practiced it, with an arsenal of psychological, emotional, and physical ploys, is seduction at its most sublime. You stay in control and get what you want.

—Greg Hartley

1.

Determine What You Need

ating and interrogation have two things in common: They bring two people together in an artificial way, and they have a purpose. You may question the latter, but dating does have a purpose—it just isn't always the same one. Depending on your life goals, your hormones, and the situation—that purpose can shape whether you simply want to have fun or head for the altar. Your date needs to be "Mr. Right for the Job." But do you know how to pick him out of the crowd? I'll help you to do just that. If you're already dating a guy, I'll show you how to figure out if you should keep him around. You will learn to D.E.C.O.D.E.:

Determine what you need.
Evaluate the pool of candidates.
Collect information about each.
Observe his behaviors.
Decide what it all means.
Emphasize positives to get the best outcome.

D.E.C.O.D.E. is a cyclic method rather than a linear one, so no matter where you are in a relationship, it's useful. Where you are in your relationship—whether you are starting to look for someone or already dating someone—will determine what part of D.E.C.O.D.E. you'll want to put your focus on.

The Dating Process

Dating, like interrogation, is a process. Unlike the way most dating occurs, though, interrogation is also a way of both understanding and managing the interaction you have with another human being. One of the first lessons I learned as an interrogator is that because there was another human involved, I could not control the entire interaction. Even so, I know how to decode human behavior, and I approach the process knowing what outcome I want. So I may not be in charge of everything, but I can direct a great deal of what goes on.

Similar to dating, interrogation starts with the question, "Does this guy have what I want, or not?" Let's take a quick look at the similarities between dating and interrogation, from beginning to end, from the first "D" to the final "E" (see table on following pages).

As you read this, you may think, "I don't need the first two steps because I'm already dating." Not so. Use the information to illuminate the reasons you acted or reacted in a certain way. Ideally, it will help you determine you have made the right choices. If you are tired of dating losers, or the same guy in a different body, you should start from the beginning and set some requirements. Keep in mind that, like interrogation requirements, life

INTERROGATION	DATING
Information collection requirements	**Determine** what you need
I go into an interrogation room knowing what kind of answers I need to questions concerning things such as troop movement or chemical weapons.	Do you haphazardly meet men and hope for good results? Or do you have requirements you're looking for in a man? Even if you think you do not have requirements—that you're open to all kinds of men—I will help you scratch deeper into your psyche and find criteria you may not even be aware of or in charge of.
Screening	**Evaluate** the pool of candidates
When I walk into a prison compound, I might have to choose among 10,000 possible interrogation subjects to find the information I need. I have to figure out which prisoners are the most likely possibilities. Based on what I can see, I say, "Those 4,000 seem to fit my needs." And then I keep narrowing the possibilities.	A single woman in New York City has a geographically convenient pool of three million men between the ages of twenty and fifty-four to choose from. If you want a Latvian ballet dancer, then you can eliminate a chunk of those right away. Sometimes I choose the wrong guy for interrogation and do not realize it until I have invested time. Sound familiar? There are ways to prevent it.
Planning and preparation	**Collect** information about each
I talk to guards who have exposure to the sources I've targeted, review any information about them, and get whatever insight I can from other prisoners.	No man walks into your life without history that will impact your relationship. Dig for background. Notice what his friends are like and what they say about him. What do clothes and grooming, speech patterns, and even car choices mean?

continued on following page

INTERROGATION	DATING
Interrogation	**Observe** his behaviors
Using a combination of interpersonal skills and conversation, I persuade the source to see things my way. The interrogation is a sort of dance of observation and projection that brings the source to my side, if only for a while.	As you interact with a man and observe his behaviors, you will draw on some learned tactics, as well as some instinctive ones, to discover who he is. Some of these tools will be simple observation; others will be well-designed ploys to get to the heart of the matter.
	Decide what it all means
	Does that missed dinner mean he has no respect, or that he just got so carried away with a project that he lost track of time? Is that a desirable trait? I will give you tools that help you make a fact-based decision. (You already have the emotional component you need to make the choice.) Will he change over time? Can he be the right guy?
Termination	**Emphasize** positives to get the best outcome
When I feel as though I've gotten everything I can get from a session, I close the interrogation. The termination process is the most important—and complex—part of the interrogation. It actually consists of multiple stages: ending the questioning session, setting the expectation for further sessions, and reinforcing what worked.	When something is working, use positive reinforcement to keep it working. All animals respond well to that, especially men. Conversely, do not give positive reinforcement to unwanted behavior.

has a tendency to change. You may find yourself moving up and down the process. Each chapter of this book has tidbits of human behavior that I have learned through trial and error in the interrogation room. As you read, think of how like your dating life the interrogation process is.

Determine What You Need

Most people think that a date starts with a first encounter with a man, but it really starts with self-examination. This involves knowing who in your life has helped shape your values, who influences you now, and what kind of person you are.

The Managers in Your Life

Unlike police interrogation, the intelligence interrogations that I have conducted were not about confession but about finding facts. In movies and television, the interrogator is the driving force; he is all-knowing and runs the show. In real life, an interrogator is only part of the machine. When I was running an interrogation, someone else told me what I was looking for. To use a showbiz analogy, the interrogator is the talent. And, like all talent, interrogators also have managers who call the shots. These people task interrogators with collection requirements.

You have managers in your life, too, and they have power over your dating choices whether you realize it or not. They help you create a clear picture of who a desirable date is. They affect your notions of concepts like *truth* and *fidelity,* as well as attributes

such as *handsome* and *successful*. That means that, in a profound
way, they are in your head saying "Yes" or "No" when you pick
a guy out of a crowd and when you're on a date with him. All of
these voices affect your decision regarding who has potential.

Exactly what is potential? Depending on who you are, and
what voices make the most noise is your head, potential could
reflect any of the following about a man:

- What he has done
- What he does
- What he might do
- What he'll never be capable of doing

Dating the captain of the football team or sleeping with a rock
star means you've realized a certain kind of potential: You are
"famous by injection." You are with him so that makes you a cut
above, too. You could also be "rich by injection" because of the
company you keep. In all cases, you have linked your potential to
another person's success, and the importance of it was probably
defined by people in your family or social group. If they didn't
value the captain of the football team, then you wouldn't either.
I can hear you saying, "That's not true! My friends and my parents hate Jimmy." Maybe so, but they still influenced your decision to be with him, even if it's out of sheer rebellion.

This behavior is distinguished from that of a woman who seeks
the company of a man who is really good at what he does, even
though he may not have realized his potential, because she can't
be with a slacker. She has a self-perception of being productive
and maybe even exceptional, so anyone who can't match her, at

least in terms of potential, holds no appeal. Again, this comes from values inculcated from family and friends.

Some women, primarily young women, see potential as an end state, meaning stored-up capability is as good as accomplishment. If a man has the script for a great novel in his head, then he is a great novelist. Other women are inclined to think of potential as part of a growth process. They have a sense of causality in evaluating a man: If he scores fifty points in a football game, then he is capable of being a war hero, a success in business, a great role model for his children. I see a person with potential as loaded with the ability to do something. Period. He may never do that something, but that doesn't diminish his ability to do it.

Finally, as an interrogator, I have a connotation of potential that's negative. If I waste my time with a source who might have potential instead of screening out the "potentials" and targeting the prisoner who knows something important, people will die.

Ask yourself: Am I going to be happy with all that potential lying on the couch?

EXERCISE 1. VOICES IN YOUR HEAD

OBJECTIVE: Turn up the volume on the voices in your head—Mom, Dad, girlfriends, celebrities, advice columnists, teachers, and preachers.

Think of the perfect man for you—the one that, if you met him tomorrow, you would dream about and fantasize about being with. Describe him in terms of the following:

O *Appearance*   O *Career*   O *Family*   O *Religion*   O *Lifestyle*

How much of your description comes from what other people have told you is "great," or "something to look for," or even "absolutely necessary"? How much of it comes from trying really hard to prove them wrong?

How You're Wired

Many of the exercises in this book loop back to help you develop a self-assessment. Let's get started on that assessment with this short quiz. If you are one of the many women who goes for sex-symbol handsome as the first element of a profile, ask yourself what the primary reason is. Here are some sample answers to that question:

1. You consider yourself attractive and know you have the ability to snag the good-looking guy.
2. You have self-esteem issues, and getting the handsome guy makes you feel better about yourself. (Calm down if this is your honest answer. In my experience, it is the most common response.)
3. You are superficial and do not care how he sounds or what he does; he just has to look great.
4. You find it easier to get to know someone if you do not have issues about his looks.

The same goes for a primary criterion of "smart," "rich," "well-educated," and so on. As long as you know why your profile starts there, you have a solid beginning.

You should be aware that none of these answers is wrong or makes you "less than." They reflect different ways of looking at the world and nothing more. You need to know honestly who you are, or you will sabotage yourself and your dating life.

None of my tricks of the trade will do you a damned bit of good if you do not have an adequate level of self-awareness. No one else needs know what you know about yourself, though. I often misrepresent my understanding of self to probe for others' awareness of me.

To start, let's begin to use the D.E.C.O.D.E. sequence. Answer a few questions honestly about what you want, so you can determine your needs.

What Are Your Basic Requirements?

Do you want him to drive you around in his Jaguar convertible? Do you want him to hold your hand in public? Do you want him to have a Ph.D. and a British accent? The answer to this can obviously change from one "him" to another. But to the best of your ability, you need to know the answer at the moment of contact. In an ideal world (at least tonight), what's your outcome?

In interrogation, when the war changes, the information requirements change. In dating, you can't work off of old requirements, either. If you do, you repeat relationships when you may need to be reinventing them. When you're twenty, you might want just want a party buddy, but by the time you reach your thirties, you might want someone to father your child. Do not cheat on figuring out your requirements, or you will waste your most valuable asset: time.

Do You Need Approval?

If you do need approval, either seriously or desperately, you'll be an easy target for a man who wants to take advantage of your emotional neediness. You must face this need for approval as you profile men you date. If you don't, you will allow the filter of need to distort your judgment so profoundly that you could easily become a victim. I'm not kidding: Most men I know can sense neediness like animals can sense an encroaching hurricane. They may not have the capability to tell you what they are sensing, but they do see vulnerability.

Set Clear Priorities

When an interrogator knows for certain what he is looking for, he can start to scan the pool of potential sources. I categorize candidates with a system that helps rank sources in order of importance and my initial take on how hard it will be to get them to talk. When it comes to dating, you do not need anything this elaborate, but you do need some system of ranking the men who will be your potential candidates.

Maryann and I interviewed women ranging in age from eighteen to fifty-five to get a sense of what they would put on a checklist of attractive physical attributes and demeanor. The lists weren't that different, and they might serve as a good starting point for you, so we have used them to create an exercise.

The combinations can be amusing, but there is no *right* answer, only your answer. So the flamboyant, athletic, truck driver with the perfect Oxford accent may be out there, or he may not, but you have a clear starting point. I know a man whose profile for the ideal woman included "five-foot-six, blonde, with a slight overbite." See? Yours is not so strange.

EXERCISE 2. SORT THINGS OUT

OBJECTIVE: The specifics of attraction will surface in this exercise.

Make a list of things that attract you to a guy before you ever talk to him. We've given you the scales of what other women have said, just to see where you fall in relation. I've assigned a 0 to 5 rating to items in the categories so that you can figure out numerically where your personal preferences lie. By the way, a 5 in every category does not define the most ideal man. In fact, he would be a weird guy who exists in bad science-fiction romances. You have to look at each criterion and ask yourself honestly what you like.

Grooming

Cleanliness _____
Example: smells like a locker room = 0; no dandruff and decent nails = 2.5; meticulous/fussy = 5
Some sense of fashion _____
Example: ripped shirt and stained armpits = 0; stuff that goes together = 2.5; dapper = 5

Masculinity

Healthy/fit _____
Example: panda-bear or gecko body = 0; fits into normal-sized clothes = 2.5; Olympian = 5
Gestures/posture _____
Example: flamboyantly expressive = 0; squared hips, relatively low movement with the arms = 5

Eloquence

Use of words _____
Example: jargon and jive = 0; easily understood = 2.5; poetic = 5
Sincerity _____
Example: likes the sound of his voice the best = 0; give and take = 2.5; every phrase is an invitation = 5

Demeanor

Confidence _____
Example: nebbish = 0; completely comfortable in his own skin = 5
Power _____
Example: feeble in spirit = 0; has an unmistakable air = 5

Features

Face _____
Example: pretty = 0; weather-beaten cowboy = 5
Stature _____
Example: your size—whatever that is = 0; the opposite of your size—whatever that is = 5
Color _____
Example: exactly what you are = 0; as far away from what you are as possible = 5

EXERCISE 3. WHAT IS MAGIC TO YOU

OBJECTIVE: Now that you know what characteristics attract you, find out what tricks you fall for.

Get together with a friend, or a group, and make a list of the little things a guy might do that immediately make him more attractive to you. Do you find his dancing appealing? How about his ability to tell jokes or shoot pool?

After that, do the opposite. Make a list of things that guys do to enhance their appeal that you find repulsive. Maryann's favorite example is a bodybuilder she knew who would strike a pose with his back flared and arms out—it's known as a lat spread—when he wanted to impress a woman.

Turn Off the Neon Sign

Once your picture of a desirable guy has taken shape, you have to learn to control yourself in front of the prospects.

As an interrogator, I would not strut into the room and ask, "Y'all don't have any weapons of mass destruction, do ya?" I can easily compromise my collection effort by telling the source I've selected what I am looking for. He will either become exactly the opposite of what I need or, to get a favor, will quickly become exactly what I do need, whether he really has the information or not. Dating is not much different. If you wear your heart on your sleeve, you will be an easy target for the unscrupulous.

Once you have determined your needs, keep them to yourself until you go through more of the D.E.C.O.D.E. process. If you don't, you give up much of your ability to figure out whether or not a potential dating prospect meets those needs.

The hard part is involuntarily telegraphing your excitement at having found "the one." I learned that lesson the hard way while

I was going through some grueling simulations to help prepare me to serve as an interrogator in the field.

Prior to one of the many interrogation exercises that were part of this training, I noticed the most attractive woman in the current class of trainees was a petite, gorgeous brunette. When the team captured me the next day, they went through the usual drill of blindfolding me, stripping off some of my clothes, and then slamming on handcuffs and barraging me with questions and taunts.

Unlike most of the others in the drill, I'd already gone through resistance training, so my body language leaked nothing. My mouth leaked nothing. And then the hot little brunette whispered in my ear, "I know who you are."

My boss got this on video, unfortunately: I softened visibly and curled down toward her face to hear her better. She had instantly elicited a response typical of us males, which is to soften when we get near a woman we're attracted to. In short, she caught me off guard, so I responded naturally instead of like a trained professional. (That never happened again.)

When you meet a man you like, how much of what you do is intentional? This is a tough question, one you probably should explore with one or two trusted friends and a bottle of wine. To supplement that conversation, try the next exercise (*on the following page*).

EXERCISE 4. DO YOU MEAN IT

OBJECTIVE: Learn about your physical indicators of sending a signal that you are attracted to someone.

Do this with at least one friend whom you trust—someone with whom you've had that conversation about "How much of what you do is intentional?" Give your friend carte blanche to pick the occasion where they will analyze you so that you aren't on your guard. And then, at some sporting event, party, or some other place where you run into someone you like, let her observe you and report back. Try not to be offended or defensive. Listen.

After your friend looks for your physical indications of attraction and tells you what she sees, pay attention to your own body language in front of someone you're attracted to. This exercise will help you intentionally use the rituals of plumage ruffling—that thing that a bird does when it wants to mate with another bird—as well as spot them more accurately in others. For example, do you always touch him when you laugh at even the lamest of jokes? Do you play with your necklace like you were in junior high?

Now you are prepared to go out and find your man the same way an interrogator would. You find out as much as you can about him—maybe even before you lay eyes on him—and then watch his interactions with those around him.

2.
Evaluate What's out There

In the screening part of an interrogation, I decide who has value.

Just like you in the dating world, interrogators are a priceless commodity. There is usually only one interrogator for dozens to thousands of possible sources, that is, people we've determined have information we want. We have to filter through those who have potential to find those who have value. In an early stage of the profiling process, interrogators learn by watching from afar and talking to people who have interacted with a prisoner of interest.

Even after we have contact with a source, we are constantly re-evaluating the rest of the pool to make sure we have the right guy. You may be in a dating relationship right now—and you may think he's the right guy for you—but you will have a much better sense of him if you go through this material anyway. At least you'll be able to answer one critical question: "Is he normal?"

Watching the Moves

Without going into great detail—I did that in my last book, *I Can Read You Like a Book*, which was all about body language—here are facts to get you started in evaluating a guy based on the way he moves. All humans share some communication traits, regardless of culture, gender, or language. I break down the elements of physical communication into four categories: illustrators, regulators, adaptors, and barriers:

ILLUSTRATORS Just as you might guess from the name, these are gestures that illustrate what you are thinking and that use your body to emphasize what you are saying. Women tend to be more demonstrative than most men (straight ones, anyway), who tend toward blocky moves. The function of illustrators is to punctuate a statement.

➤ **EXAMPLES** finger pointing; head bobbing; using the hand, arm, or head like a baton; outstretching arm with palm up, as if to suggest you are giving something; rolling the eyes; shrugging shoulders.

REGULATORS This term describes body language that is used to control a conversation, specifically another person's speech. Men are woefully inadequate at this compared to women. You can easily master "talk to the hand." Or picture this: eyes closed, head thrown back, nose in the air. Remember, context is everything, so unless you are naked and horizontal, the signal is the unmistakable question, "Why are you even bothering to talk to me?" A gentler signal would be touching someone to let her know you are not quite finished; please be quiet. The sharp cut of the eyes that means "Just shut up" anchors the other end of the spectrum. If you've just left a relationship that lasted months or years, you likely developed a vocabulary of regulators and have some of them left over as baggage. A new guy may not get them immediately, so do not expect that he will.

▶ **EXAMPLES** putting a hand up like a stop sign; putting a finger to the lips to ask for silence; moving the hand quickly in a circle as a way of saying, "Speed it up."

ADAPTORS These gestures serve to relieve stress. When you are uncomfortable, the nervous energy has to go somewhere. From compulsive self-grooming to petting your hair and neck, people use adaptors to adapt to a stressful environment. Men tend to take a more aggressively tactile approach (surprised?) with their adaptors than women. Women also use a specific set of adaptors in a situation of sexual attraction, such as tilting the head, touching the neck, or petting or twirling the hair—a dead giveaway to the trained eye. People often develop idiosyncratic adaptors, which usually look very different depending on whether a man or a woman is doing them. They are too numerous to list; we simply recognize them in a category called ticks. You know them when you see them now; you know they are ways to deal with nervous energy. Open your eyes and you can see the cause. Maybe it's you!

▶ **EXAMPLES COMMON TO WOMEN** stroking; scratching lightly; shifting; wiggling a foot; soft, petting movements on the arm.

▶ **EXAMPLES COMMON TO MEN** wringing hands; rubbing thighs; picking at nails in monkey-like fashion.

BARRIERS These gestures are meant to separate you from another person. Barriers may be symbolic, such as interlacing the fingers, or physical, such as hiding behind a couple of unwelcoming friends. They are a way to block you from an interloper. Whether you intend it or not, using a barrier is powerful. A variation on this in flirtation is using the brow as a barrier in a playful way: Put your head down, with your eyes looking up in a childlike manner. You are concurrently blocking and inviting.

▶ **EXAMPLES** computer bag, desk, podium, arms, newspaper, beer bottle, other people.

Stress Moves

When stress levels increase, the stressed person's behavior changes. In each of the four types of body language, increased stress is shown in a particular way.

ILLUSTRATORS GO FROM SMOOTH TO ERRATIC When you talk and use your hands to emphasize your thoughts naturally, the two are synchronized. When you are under stress, the brain will still try to emphasize what it is thinking. The result is choppy body language that seems to be out of synch with the conversation.

REGULATORS MAY BECOME EMPHATIC A violent head shake or extreme head tilt in an effort to silence someone, for example, sends a strong message that the person has anxiety about the conversation; it needs to take a different turn right now. This is especially true for someone who is normally polite and suddenly becomes emphatic about stopping the conversation.

ADAPTORS BECOME MORE PRONOUNCED For example, if a guy tends to rub his arm because he's a little uncomfortable, he might push his sweatshirt sleeve up, rub his arm, shove his shirt sleeve back down, and repeat the process if the discomfort is more extreme. Under stress, we all manage to release energy. When I was a younger man with a lot more hair, I would run my hand backward over my hair as if smoothing it. I have noticed other men doing the same. (Now I find it takes me less time to smooth my hair.)

BARRIER INTENSITY OR FREQUENCY WILL INCREASE People are rarely aware of barriers. Watch people in your daily life use barriers, whether intentionally or not. As the unwanted intensity of a situation increases, so will the frequency of putting up barriers. It is a sign that the person wants space. I might ask a friend, "How did your date go?" If he gives me a blow-by-blow that begins with, "We sat down and she put her bag on the table," the story does not usually end well. Whether she knew it or not, she put up a barrier at the start of the date. Know this and use it to send the message you plan—not one that happens inadvertently.

As you can see from these descriptions, stress moves are deviations from what is normal for a person. You may find that "normal" for your neurotic Prince Charming is anything but calm and relaxed. You can easily mistake a high-energy young man with a cross-legged foot flail for someone who is uneasy and not at peace in his skin. For some people, flirting creates so much anxiety that their stress indicators project a really distorted impression. So when you're in this "evaluate" stage of D.E.C.O.D.E., watch a guy before you have personal contact with him. Try to see what's normal for *him*.

I've known guys who tense up like that, and some of them deny they have any ability to flirt or even any understanding of the dynamics of flirting. The best way to explain flirtation is by beginning with the phrase "flirting with disaster." Take skydiving as an example. Every time a person does it, she is beating the odds; she pushes the envelope of safety.

Similarly, flirting is an act that pushes the envelope of human interaction. Every time you flirt, you test the waters, just like an interrogator balancing anxiety with comfort for his source. If you flirt with someone with the intent of more substantial contact, you will push the envelope more than if you flirt without that intent.

Think of it as personal jeopardy: If I am only playing, with no intent of short- or long-term benefit other that the play itself, I expose myself to less risk. On the other hand, if I have vested interest (the desire for sex for the evening or long-term romance), I place my ego in a little more jeopardy. It's analogous to a first skydive: You have some sense of putting yourself at risk, but you have a strong desire to do it anyway. That perception of risk, no matter how slight, can engender some stress responses.

One of the easiest things to learn is how other people react to different kinds of stress. It is easiest when you are not involved with the person. In the following exercise, you will detach yourself from other people's stress and just be a fly on the wall with eyes open. You may even learn something you thought you already knew about human beings. As you go through this next exercise on detecting stress, primarily you will want to note extremes in the types of body language I've categorized as illustrators, regulators, adaptors, and barriers.

EXERCISE 5. BODY SCAN FOR STRESS

OBJECTIVE: Learn what stress looks like on other people.

Pick a venue where you can spend some time watching other people, preferably a place where human interaction would be expected of someone. A bar or a party would be better options than a shopping mall or church service. Focus on the men in the crowd. Watch for changes in their behavior as first encounters take place—particularly first encounters with women. Look for signs such as the following:

- Choppy movements when the level of discomfort is high. Humans adapt as they grow accustomed to the new stimulus, so this is something you are likely to notice in the very beginning of an encounter.
- Increased use of adaptors
- Use of barriers
- Overly blocky appearance. Most men know that flared shoulders and feet shoulder-width apart presents a masculine image. But you and I both know—without an interrogator's education—that some men play the role of "manly man" by adopting the posture because they have something to hide, like a weak self-image. (Translation: They are scared to death of you and overcompensate with the macho thing.) As an interrogator, I may have seen this more than you. When they are intimidated, men adopt a posture with attitude or try to show off. They desperately want *someone* to think they have a powerful center, a formidable presence. Right.

As the comfort level rises, you will notice that a man's mannerisms and gestures start to become more like those of the person he is talking to. This mirroring is normal; we all do it. Some people are more natural than others, and the mirroring process moves faster. The key here is to start to get a comfort level with understanding real human behavior and identifying its components. These will all come into play as you decode your date later. The more you do this, the sooner it will become second nature.

What makes George Clooney "the sexiest man alive"? It's far more than his face. Paradoxically, a big part of his attractiveness and persona is what he doesn't show—stress. People like George Clooney are never merely comfortable *in* an environment; they are comfortable *at* the environment. If he goes into a truck stop on the New Jersey Turnpike, he isn't in the truck stop; the truck stop is around him. He carries with him the identity of George Clooney; he is not just a restaurant patron named George Clooney.

My persona is interrogator; I carry it with me. It's my invisible Darth Vader costume. I use it to change the air around me when I go somewhere, rather than have the air change me.

The Power of Presence

Whether celebrities are politicians, actors, singers, or athletes, they have power. This power affects everyday people because we have a difficult time explaining it. It makes average people feel tongue-tied—they fill space with inane chatter—because they do not feel their own presence is quite enough to the fill the space. When Mel Gibson was in Columbus, Georgia, filming *We Were Soldiers,* my old friend Walt saw him working out in the gym. Walt wanted to say something to Mel, so he tried to find common ground. Like most of us, Walt has little in common with someone like Mel, so he tried what seemed natural: "Are you homesick?"

Mel either did not understand Walt or was simply trying to distance himself. He looked at Walt quizzically: "Did you ask me if I'm a homosexual?" I told Walt he probably has the distinction of being the only straight man to hit on Mel Gibson in a gym.

Walt's attempt was actually a very enlightened way to deal with the situation, that is, to try and find common ground. Humans all have something in common. Many people in Walt's situation might feel a bit of stress thinking of what to say to such a big celebrity. What would you say?

If you find that you're like my friend, it's a sign that you should pay close attention to the exercises in the book. Most of them will help you overcome the power that *presence* gives certain people, whether from their looks or status. By the end of this book, you will be able to recognize their vulnerabilities as they surface in adaptors, barriers, and so on. Similarly, you will have that advantage with members of the opposite sex.

To help you get there, here are some interrogator-like extreme self-awareness and adaptation skills.

You probably chose a comfortable setting for your people-watching in the previous exercise. That's natural. But what if the kind of guy you want tends to hang out in places where you don't feel comfortable—in the bowling alley, at a country bar or church event, or at the opera? How are you going to evaluate the pool of candidates when you are the one most likely to show stress (and maybe give away your motivation for being there)?

Interrogators start by learning the customs, as well as the language, of people they will be interrogating. Young interrogators are forced into intense role-play exercises hundreds of times before their first contact with a prisoner. Life involves a lot less rehearsal, but you can still achieve the same end of raising your comfort level in strange situations. Exposure is the key. The more you do something, the easier it becomes.

What gets anyone to the point of showing stress? Displaced expectation. When you are not the master (or mistress) in a figurative sense of all you survey, then you will feel some discomfort. Depending on your personality and how far you are from being in control of your environment, you will show signs of stress ranging from the barely perceptible to the very obvious.

All people have anxiety in a completely new environment, because if you have not been exposed to it before, you can't master it—no matter how gutsy or clever you are. A new situation—like a first date—forces you to adapt. At my age and with my diverse life experiences, far fewer situations make me uncomfortable than when I was a high school boy in Georgia, but they are still out there.

Women commonly show discomfort by exhibiting the following behaviors:

- Physically moving toward a friend, or toward something familiar. Even clutching a purse is a sign that the woman is trying to claim her own real estate.
- Blotching in the neck, or perhaps some blushing
- Adaptors (as described on page 17), also known as *comfort habits*
- Looking around more than usual
- Touching the nose a lot and maybe scratching it
- Vocal cues, such as sarcasm, for example, if the person feels stress, or a change in the pace or tone of the person's speech

EXERCISE 6. SELF-EXAM FOR STRESS

OBJECTIVE: Learn what stress looks like on you.

Along with a friend, go somewhere you've never been before and see what your signs of discomfort are. You can go to a church service that's unfamiliar to you, preferably one that has definite rituals, such as Catholic. Try to fit in. Or you could visit a strip bar, a country bar, or some other bar where you would ordinarily never venture. Try to fit in.

Look for your indicators of stress, such as those listed on the facing page. You and your friend should rate your stress response to the strange environment on a scale from 0 to 5, with 5 indicating a spastic reaction. The closer you are to 0, the more comfortable you will be taking control of a conversation.

Moving toward something familiar. . . . . _____
Blotching or blushing . . . . _____
Adaptors (comfort habits). . . . . _____
Looking around . . . . _____
Touching the nose . . . . _____
Vocal cues . . . . _____

Important note: Do this exercise with a friend, and if you get far past your comfort level, step away. You need to know what your tolerance level is for a given situation, and then push yourself in degrees. You don't want to break out in hives. The real magic of this self-enhancement exercise is learning not to telegraph your needs, unless it is by choice. Try this exercise in a couple of different settings so that you and your friend can compare notes on what stress looks like—in you and her.

As you stretch your ability to deal with foreign situations, you will find yourself able to handle an ever-widening range of circumstances without showing stress. You might even develop a kind of presence, or air, that adds to your distinction. At the very least, you won't be as intimidated as you may have been before by someone else's air of distinction.

Every time you go into a new situation, push the envelope a little bit, and leave. Know that everyone else there probably had a similar discomfort level when they first went to that particular place. After you do this exercise in enough places, you will start to put the "strangeness" into perspective and cope with it differently.

The goal of the last two exercises is to help you be better able to evaluate the pool of candidates by building up your ability to do the following:

- Understand what the indicators of stress are both in him and in you. Some stress is actually *good*; it means you're excited about being with the person. It can keep you on your toes, ready to run toward him—or away from him.
- Find the limits of your social comfort zone.
- Notice when signs of stress kick in and what those signs are so you can manage these indicators for self-protection.

"Sexy" Moves

The body language I'm about to cover is often more humorous than it is sexy, but that's certainly not the intent of the person doing it.

When men are in the company of other men vying for the same woman, or pool of women, they will display hyper-masculine behavior, which may look incongruous because they are somewhat uncomfortable. A woman will become hyper-feminine under analogous circumstances—and by that I do not mean girly, per se. I mean whatever her idea of feminine is; if she "plays against type," it's probably a sign that she is nervous. Consider the women in *Sex and the City*, who become hyper-feminine by spotlighting their respective strengths: Samantha goes sexier, Charlotte becomes more artsy, Miranda uses her intellect, and Carrie sharpens her wit. When Miranda tries to become Samantha,

EXERCISE 7. PROSPECTING

> **OBJECTIVE:** Pay attention to an attractive guy's body language to see if it makes him more or less attractive to you.

Watch a man you have an interest in *before* he even knows you exist or are in the room. You want to know how he behaves without an agenda that involves you. Use a list like the one below that covers first impression, overall movement, arms and hands, feet and legs, and posture to evaluate your mark:

First impression: What is the most distinct thing about him? If you are like most humans, the first thing you are going to notice is the thing that makes a man attractive to you, or the absence of it. Look past this for a moment as you build a head-to-toe list of who he is, not who he isn't. Start with overall impressions.

Overall movement:

Blocky ——————————————————————— Fluid

Where does he fit on this scale? If more to the blocky side, then he presents a more traditional male image. Find yourself really attracted to men who seem to swagger? The design of the male body makes it well suited to swaggering. Maybe you prefer more graceful movements. That is a learned style for men, but don't conclude it's gay. Some manly men have elegance in their moves, rather than a swagger. Other men who had a strong female role model may turn into the momma's boy and be very feminine in most behaviors—except for the one that makes the difference between gay and straight. Somewhere in the middle is where most of us live. The extremely blocky presentation may mean nothing more than the person feels threatened or outclassed in the dating scene and strives for a hyper-masculine look to rise above the competition. He is ruffling plumage. If this happens in an office or other work environment, he is likely in the presence of men he sees as superior. At any rate, chances are good he has no idea what he's doing—but you do.

continued on following page

EXERCISE 7 CONTINUED

Arms and hands:

Composed ————————————————————————————— Flailing

If the group he is part of includes other males, look at others in the group. How demonstrative are his arm movements as opposed to theirs? At this point, you want a sense of his subculture and whether he feels a need to mirror behavior of others in his group or perhaps even to be the one the others mirror. This exercise invites you to look at men in a context, as well as to look at a man individually.

Is anyone (especially him) wildly flailing like a TV mobster? This is even more telling because men typically flail only when there is a passionate conversation. Keep in mind that if you are in New York City, flailing is different from "flailing" in St. Paul, Minnesota. One possible reason why he may be more demonstrative than others in his group is that he is a transplant from a location where big gestures are common. I see this all the time because I live in Atlanta, which is Transplant City; the norm is all over the board.

Other gestures to watch for are use of his index finger to beat the air, closing his hand as if he were holding a whip, or expressing a concept with his hands as though he were playing charades. This kind of gesturing can indicate passion about a topic—upper arms rising as high as parallel to the ground while hands gesticulate—but you need to know that elbows constantly rising above shoulders may mean his dream date has chest hair. A sampling of other telling signs includes these:

- From personal training and experience, I can tell you that military men point with their entire hand: thumb pulled in and all fingers illustrating a direction or site of interest. Then again, he could be just copying someone else's style. All of these factors play into your quest for knowledge about who he is, and the richer your profiling skills become, the faster you will make sense out of them.
- Does the man hook his thumbs in his belt? This masculine gesture can actually come from necessity. If the man is a cop, his training and instincts tell him to keep his hands close to his firearm. I watched armed security personnel at a huge festival and saw this posture replicated over and over.

continued on following page

- Is he handling the invisible ring? Either he has just ended the relationship or he is still in the relationship and just checking the status of the wedding band. I have known soldiers who put rings on dog-tag chains and constantly checked the ring with a pat on the chest. As a corollary, when you take off something that has been there for a long time—or even a short time in which you felt a strong emotional connection—you will show signs of missing it.

- The classic male adaptor is wringing his hands as he walks into a new and uncomfortable place. It looks as though he has just finished washing his hands. It you see that, it just means he's a little nervous.

- The fig leaf—what I call "protecting the precious"—is another male barrier you have seen through the years in all settings: hands crossed in front of the genitals. Some men do versions of this with the added "protection" of an object such as a briefcase, raincoat, bottle of beer, or newspaper. You have your own version of protecting the precious, as well: pointing your toes inward in sexual submission. Men may do that under great psychological duress, but it is a distinctly female move.

- A man's adjusting himself is a generic sign of maleness. Don't read too much into it.

Make your own list. Categorize what you see in terms of illustrators, regulators, adaptors, and barriers. Follow the same process as you watch a man's legs, feet, and the way he stands and walks. Hands are humans' first tools, and we show it. Look for signs of restlessness, dominance, and even compromise in the hands of the man you are watching from afar.

Legs and feet:

Open ————————————————————————— Guarded

Legs can serve as an invitation or a barrier; they can display confidence or high stress. Watch a man sit to learn about his state of mind. Crossed legs cause all kinds of wrong conclusions. Forget the litany of interpretations about this when you watch a man. Some men cross their legs high, with an ankle resting on the other thigh, because their legs are big and muscular. Some men are so muscular and inflexible that they do not cross their legs; you see them sit with their legs apart. Some men can assume the European look of tightly crossed legs.

continued on following page

EXERCISE 7 CONTINUED

Just check out his anatomy before you draw conclusions about what his leg crossing means.

Relaxed ——————————————————————— Agitated

- When a man sits on a chair or bar stool and strokes his thighs, he is trying to adapt to a situation. It's just an autoerogenous gesture that helps him feel more comfortable. Think baseball batter on deck.
- Men and women both release energy—an adaptive process—by moving toes and feet. Think of how you rub one foot on another or tap your foot or curl your toes when you feel nervous. Men do the same kinds of things.
- Look for anything that looks like nervous energy release. Note: Do not mistake normally high energy levels for stress. Some men, especially young ones, have high energy levels. Find out what is normal for the individual. You'll find more on that in the section on baselining (page 62).
- Look for choppy patterns of movement. People who are uncomfortable have a tendency to choppiness or erratic movement.

Posture:

Confrontational ——————————————————————— Relaxed

Remember the last time you saw a snarling, growling dog? Maybe another dog looked threatening. A man can be the same way: Any one of a number of things, including one too many beers, will set him off. Unless men have a confrontational nature (watch out), they position themselves obliquely to other men and face-on to women. If you see two heterosexual men get close and face to face, they are likely being secretive. When men are secretive, one of the men will likely serve as a barrier for the other. Look for ways the person uses barriers, such as holding a beer bottle in front of him and peeling the label for "something to do." Does he stand with hips tucked forward, shoulders thrown out, chin up, with weight evenly distributed on both feet? Here is a man combining barriers with ruffling plumage. Watch how people move around him before you conclude he's "the man," though. Do his buddies display the same level of masculinity as he does, or are they doing the rooster strut in front of him? If guys strut around him and he behaves normally, he is likely the alpha of the group—the guy they look up to. Contrast this with the man who uses the same barriers but seems to lack a spine. He is combining barriers with shyness and/or lack of confidence. Others around him probably won't defer to him.

you know she's anxious about the encounter and is bound for disaster. The same is true for men. Some men understand that being masculine is simply being comfortable in their own skin. Others play against type, from acting more feminine to strutting like a rooster; some of them do not have a clue what they are doing or trying to do. Look for deviations from that person's normal behavior to know when he is adopting a character he thinks you *want* to see versus being a genuine prick. The man who is comfortable with women will likely show little stress, while the less experienced man will show dramatic signs of stress. It's like blushing. As your breadth of experience increases, it will probably happen less often.

Intel

The first step in screening the pool—the low-scrutiny look from a distance—is more than just a cursory glance. As an interrogator, I use this step to collect "free" information, that is, whatever I can learn without committing to the individual. I can get a sense of his place in the prison hierarchy, not only with the prisoners but also with the guards. I can look at his clothing and what he was wearing when he came in to get a strong sense of what he does for a living and how he lives.

When you apply these skills to evaluating your prospect, you can find out who he is as defined by a set of externals: How does he interact in his natural environment? How does he see himself, and what do others appear to think of him?

Interrogators actually say to themselves, "Do I want to dance with him?" I can make that decision by simply watching, but I will make a better decision by moving to the next stage. Watching from a distance only gives me a few pieces of the puzzle. Once I think I have the right guy, I start adding questions to my evaluation efforts. I ask the prisoners he associates with about him, as well as the guards, to get to know as much as possible without actually asking him anything. The people around him will help me find out what he's like and uncover the relevant details of his story and behavior. One of the main pieces of information I look for is the circumstance of capture. What brought him to this particular place at this particular time?

You need to ask questions that give you that answer and other basic facts about the guy. Nosy? Yes. Smart? Yes. After all, as I said before, you are a valuable commodity, just like an interrogator. You can't afford to go around wasting time on every guy with "potential."

3.

Collect Information
and Start Profiling

He looks like the right guy. He can handle himself socially; other people seem to respect him. Now let's give him a little closer scrutiny.

Collecting information—the "C" in D.E.C.O.D.E.— requires you to unleash your curiosity while you engage your brain. The paradox for most women in that you have this wonderfully intuitive brain that you simply refuse to use. You tend to believe what a guy says, take his actions at face value, and then engage your brain by making excuses for bad behavior and praising him for whatever he does right. You either project what you need and he takes advantage of it, or you project onto him what you want to see. (Stop it!) At the same time, you have a deep well of questions about his motives, his true nature, and his potential.

I'll go back to my world of interrogation to get you centered on how this process needs to work.

Physical Criteria

Once we narrow down the pool of candidates, interrogators begin collecting specific information about our sources by taking note of grooming, demeanor, and costume/trappings. We ask guards and others around a source to tell us about him: Does he talk to other prisoners? Does he read? Does he pray? Does he wash? Does he comply easily or is he a major pain in the ass? When a guard treats him especially well, is he grateful, or does he act like he expects it?

Now that you've determined what you need and want in a date, you're ready to start making judgments based on some of these same criteria. You'll be looking at things such as grooming and how neat he is, for instance, what kind of shoes he wears and whether or not he shines them. You will also collect basic information about who he is, all the while avoiding the novice interrogator's trap of making the person into the one you need. Watch him behave and ask questions about what you don't understand, at all times observing carefully and realizing he has biases, needs, and filters associated with what he is seeing as well.

Grooming

We all make assessments based on grooming, whether the environment is professional or recreational. Grooming reflects regular effort; it isn't something you do on Thursday night and then forget about the rest of the week. For example, a man's hands can reflect years of physical labor or sports, and yet he can convey the fact that he is well-groomed and intelligent. You may be someone who doesn't mind a guy who grooms randomly while you're dating; if so, keep in mind that you won't be able to ask him to change later, when you live with him and see him every day. What you see is what you get, or you will drive him, and yourself, crazy trying to change him.

Be careful not to confuse grooming and taste. A man might have a good eye for colors and styles and still not meet your standards in simple ways like washing his hair regularly. Would you rather see bling and current styles on your guy than have confidence that he's showered in the past twenty-four hours?

Grooming is complex. Our grooming styles come from how we perceive ourselves, as well as from external influences. A few years in the military forever changes someone's bearing and grooming. Some lash out and grow hair to the waist, while others maintain the close-cropped hair of their military stint for the rest of their lives. That is simply one of many factors that can affect a man. As you watch, ask yourself questions like these: Why did he choose that hairstyle? Is he a nail biter? What does that say about his state of comfort? Does he have a simple hair style that reflects a physically active man, or is it a carefully coiffed rugged look—stubble on his chin, but styling gel in his hair?

When I lived in New Jersey, I had a friend who was a plumber. Everyone makes jokes about plumbers' appearances, between the grease on their hands and the butt cracks showing. This guy was better groomed and neater than any soldier I knew. Women would get into his truck and comment at how astounded they were at his tidiness. The lesson? Career choice has some impact on grooming but it is not necessarily defining.

People who are overly obsessed with details will be meticu-lous, and for them, everything has its place. That may be really sexy to you if you just split up with a pig, but is the opposite extreme going to make you crazy, too? Most meticulous people have that same trait in how they see life. Do you want the guy who sees only black and white, or shades of gray?

Our grooming telegraphs how we see not only ourselves but also the world around us.

Demeanor

In observing a prisoner, interrogators look at how he behaves alone and in a group. We need to know how he interacts with oth-ers to see his impression of self, as well as others' impressions of him. This is how we decide whether or not he fits our needs.

If you have an interest in someone, watch him when he isn't with you. This isn't spying or prying; it's common sense.

Pay attention to a guy's demeanor in both normal and unusual circumstances. "Normal" would be walking his dog or hanging out in the break room at work. "Unusual" is a relative term; it's whatever is unusual for him. If you know he's a bowling-alley kind of guy, for example, and you run into him at a production of *Romeo and Juliet,* that would constitute unusual. If he is a nerdy, stay-at-home type and you see him in a bar with the guys from work, then that's unusual.

Adjusting your demeanor can be simply part of putting your-self in charge, an attempt to control events and the flow of con-versation by adopting a different role. So if the guy you're keeping your eye on has a demeanor in an unusual setting that seems incongruous with his personality, he may just be trying to adapt. You might want to cut him a break after you stop laughing.

Here are a few thoughts on collecting useful information about a guy by watching his demeanor:

- How does his dog respond to him? If his dog cowers in fear, he probably has a harsh streak.
- Humans defer to those they see as superior. Unfortunately, if someone comes across as superior to you in one environment or in one particular activity, you probably have a tendency to defer to him in another, unrelated setting. We take pain-relief advice from guys who get to remind us, "I am not a doctor, but I play one on TV." Lots of emotions can cause the deference—fear or respect, for example. You need to raise your awareness of your response.
- Is he kind or harsh to those he has power over, whether it's a junior associate in his business or a waitress? How a person treats those who have no recourse is a window into his soul. More on this later as well. (See Chapter 9.)
- Is he sarcastic at inappropriate times?
- How many regulators does he use in conversation with family, friends, coworkers, bosses, and subordinates?
- What do his illustrators look like? Are they kind, Mr. Rogers–type illustrators, or does he use the over-the-top whipping motion of Adolph Hitler?
- How much control does he exercise over his environment? He may routinely take small steps to "improve" it by moving your water glass from the edge of a counter, for example, or he may need so much control he rearranges your furniture

while you're in the bathroom. At what point do you find
those gestures annoying, rather than helpful?

- How temperamental does he become over loss of control?
- How does his rebellion surface: in passive-aggressive gestures, or in directly confrontational actions? The passive-
aggressive personality is the guy who drives the speed limit
in the left-hand lane simply because he can. When you tell
him you did not appreciate his rearranging your furniture,
he'll say, "I'm sorry," and then drag your couch to its original position—leaving a groove in your hardwood floor.

Costume/Trappings

The phrase "all hat and no cattle" has become a way for politicians from cowboy country to attack one another on credibility
issues. Make it yours, too, in evaluating whether or not the man
and his outfit work in harmony. Interrogators can freely change
rank and uniforms to get across the image they are trying to por-
tray. (A notable exception is pretending to be a Red Cross worker,
which is strictly forbidden by the Geneva Conventions.) People
do this every day.

If the Wharton MBA you have your eye on needs to be an
authority figure to his sales team, he might wear a suit in front
of them, even if it's casual Friday. But the Wharton MBA who
climbed Everest last spring might achieve the same kind of commanding presence by wearing hiking pants on casual Friday. The
costume has to match the role to have maximum effect.

Is the guy you lust after wearing sweat pants and a shredded
tank top to a company picnic? He might look buff, but his inap-

propriate attire should tell you that he either doesn't want to fit in or that he has no idea how to fit in. In either case, he has issues.

When I see someone who is very muscular wearing totally inappropriate clothes, I immediately sense insecurity. He is using what he has and may have no other value to present. He is putting his best foot, or bicep, forward. Sometimes, instead of clothes, a guy will use his car or electronic gadgets to establish his identity.

Does the guy play a guitar in public places? Always have a bike attached to the back of his car? Dress like P. Diddy when he's in a bar? Wear his iPod earphones almost all the time? These are all costumes and trappings that might be any of the following:

- Real and part of the person
- A gimmick to make him feel more comfortable, an ice-breaker. He may be using the gadget or clothes to give you a reason to say, "Hi." It could be much worse, though: It's possible he lacks real value and is trying to add some.
- Straight manipulation. Maybe he figured out that his chances of scoring with women in a music-loving crowd are excellent if he shows off his guitar playing.

Factual Criteria

Just as I quiz prison guards about potential sources, you need to quiz the people who know about your man of interest. Is it unfair? By whose rules? Whose life is it, anyway?

Let's say you enter a party and see two men. The one on the left is wearing a bow tie and has wire-rimmed glasses, a slightly receding hairline, and a reserved smile. The one on the right has a perfect smile, sharp cheekbones, slightly curly hair, playful eyes, and an open collar on his shirt. They both appear to have good physiques. Which one appeals to you more?

You think, "The guy on the right is really handsome, definitely better looking than the guy on the left, but the guy on the left has an appealing intensity. I think I'll talk to people who know them and find out more about them." Armed with a handful of questions that relate to things you would really like to know about a guy before you date him, you start asking around. You want to know things that reflect your values and interests. These are precisely the kinds of questions that people ask during speed dating, by the way. Good questions, but unfortunately, too many women believe that good answers automatically signal relationship potential:

- Was he a good student?
- What kind of kid was he? Boy Scout? Gang member?
- Does he do any volunteer work?
- What are his politics like?
- Did he go to college?
- Does he like kids?

The guy on the right (Mr. Perfect Smile) was a good student who went on to college and then law school. He was a Boy Scout. He had some experience campaigning for the Washington State Republican Party and worked as a volunteer at a Seattle suicide crisis center. Never talks about kids one way or the other. The guy on the left (Mr. Bow Tie) was a good student who studied law

EXERCISE 8. WHAT IS THE DEFERENCE

OBJECTIVE: These quick, interrelated activities focus your attention on how much you stick to your criteria in choosing a guy and how much others influence you.

First, make a list of different types of male celebrities and ask yourself who attracts you. For starters, rank the following stars in order of attractiveness:

Usher . . . . _____
Casey Affleck . . . . _____
Leonardo DiCaprio . . . . _____
George Clooney . . . . _____
Wilmer Valderrama . . . . _____

Name the single quality about your number one that most attracts you. Now look critically at why you think that. Ask yourself, "If I met him at a local garage while we were both waiting for our cars, and he were not famous, what would I think?"

Step two is to pinpoint an actor, politician, or other well-known person—it could be someone well known in just your community—that, according to your gut, you shouldn't be attracted to, based on his appearance or demeanor, but you are anyway. Why? Explain your reasons to a friend and listen to her reaction.

Do this final one with a friend. Pick someone the two of you do not think is attractive and see how other women react when you treat him as an attractive man. (Careful: Your exercise involves respect and interest, not toying with someone's emotions. You may actually discover how interesting an "unattractive" man can be.)

in Europe and then went into politics. He didn't belong to the Boy Scouts or anything like that. He's totally into international relations, human rights, and other big issues. He and his ex-wife have a son. "Oh, that's just great," you conclude, "he's divorced and boring." You dismiss the bow tie guy. After all, the other one is really handsome, smart, and well rounded. All the other guy seems to care about is serious issues that normal people can't do anything about. The cute guy probably doesn't talk about kids because he isn't sure if wants them.

The guy on the right—and here I'm describing the way he looked when he was arrested in Aspen, Colorado—is Ted Bundy, serial killer. He probably wouldn't have talked about kids because some of his victims were very young females.

On the left, you have José Manuel Ramos Horta, the way he looked when he accepted a Nobel Peace Prize in 1996. Current Prime Minister of East Timor and a long-time peace activist, he did not have much time for extracurricular activities. In short, the prime minister is a much better option if you're a sane woman.

I am not saying that attractiveness in a movie-land way is a lousy filter or that asking background questions is pointless. I am saying that you have to build your criteria from your completed self-assessment so that the other person's good looks and other major traits fit into a context for you. Never lose sight of what you've determined you want in a man. Your vision may change— that's normal—but it should not change every ten minutes, depending on who's better looking than whom.

You need to discover what a particular man really offers you, not just what you *think* he offers you. When you're collecting information about a guy, you might come up with a two-dimensional sketch with a three-line caption. He might have the endorsement of people you trust at work or of a couple of girlfriends, but you don't know enough about him at this stage to know if you should date him.

In each instance here, your initial attraction or lack of attraction probably came from superficial assessments: grooming, demeanor, costume/trappings, and a few basic facts. Some women get so carried away with this small amount of information that they're ready to say "Yes!" to anything. If that's you, then now, at least you're aware of it.

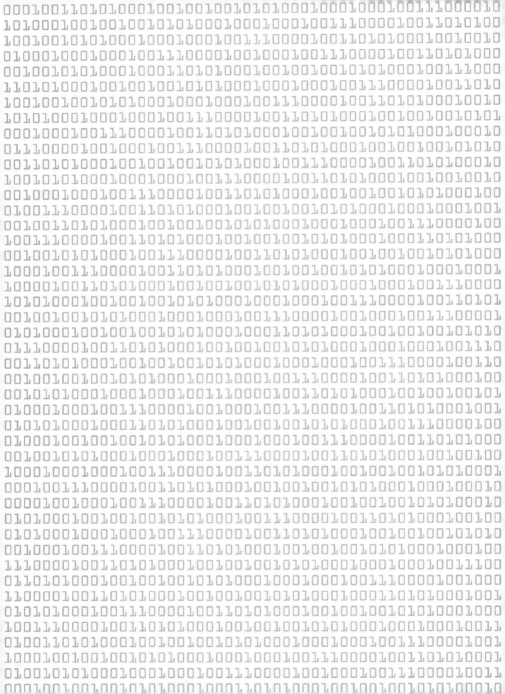

4.

Observe: Prepare
for Contact

In the interrogation world, it is possible to pick the wrong "dance partner." Despite all of the objective selection criteria I've used to evaluate a source, I might still project on him what I want to see. I get him into the interrogation room and keep projecting: "He's the man. He's the one I need." Suddenly, I realize that I've got the wrong guy.

What I want to do is give you tools that stop you from inviting the wrong guy to the dance. If you're already dancing with the wrong guy, these tools will help you recognize the mismatch and get out now.

So, from this point on in D.E.C.O.D.E., your focus is on a particular man, either someone you are already dating or someone you have an interest in.

Redefining "Observe"

Interrogation is a complex process. It includes simple observation of behaviors and responses, as well as complex tools to get someone to behave the way you want him to. In the dating context, I want you to think of the "observe" portion of the D.E.C.O.D.E. process as more than just watching. It also includes interpretative, and even manipulative, portions of the interrogator's skill set.

You will begin with passive observation, but while you're doing it, you will use some interrogation skills—and I will teach you lots of them—to know what his behavior means. Then, when you feel certain you are ready, you will use some high-end tricks to elicit behaviors that will tell you exactly who you are dealing with.

Remember how uncomfortable and nervous you felt doing Exercise 6, in which you induced a stress reaction in yourself? Your control over your responses was not exactly ideal. Remember how other people behaved when you watched them in stressful situations? Keep these thoughts in the forefront of your mind because now they will become the foundation of your observation skills. At the core of your observation is pinpointing glitchy behavior—anything that screams, "He has issues!"

You can begin to figure that out by discerning the following:

- Whether he talks *to* you or *at* you
- How he ruffles his plumage—for you and other women
- His default response to situations and people (positive or negative?)
- His self-perception
- His conflict style (When he's a little threatened or when something happens and he isn't in control, how does his behavior change?)
- His manners

Talking To *or* At

Storytelling is talking *at*, not talking *to*, a person. In some cases, a guy talking *at* you is just trying to fill space, but in others, he could not care less about you.

In an interrogation, talking *at* a source is just a shot over the bow rather than a consistent way of relating. I would not talk *at* a source (a prisoner) because I need to get into his head. Conversely, a source may be trying to talk *at* me as part of a shielding mechanism.

A man who talks *at* you gives you superficial knowledge of himself, at best, and invites no significant information about you. Conversely, a man who talks *to* you is trying to know something about you. There is a give and take.

All good talk-show hosts and interviewers talk *to* people, not *at* them. Larry King, Oprah, and Ellen are excellent examples, which is why they keep winning awards. The audience feels comfortable with them because their guests feel comfortable with them.

Plumage Ruffling

When a woman preens while making eye contact, a man considers that flattering. A man may not consciously identify the hair flipping, head tilt, and girlish laugh as seductive behavior, but he perceives it on some level.

Cavemen had this down: You are attractive. I am stronger, so we have a date. In our non-caveman world, this flow of events is potentially felonious behavior. Today, *you* have control over your willingness to date, making you a vital commodity. It's probably

EXERCISE 9. TO YOU OR AT YOU

OBJECTIVE: Identify when a man is talking to initiate a give-and-take conversation versus when he is talking without inviting any input from you.

You can do this exercise alone or with a friend. Please keep in mind that I will ask you to return to this exercise after I share a few other skills with you—so don't speculate about what's next at this stage. Just stick with the basics.

Initiate a conversation with a man you're interested in, or allow yourself to be engaged in a conversation. This should be in a setting where you are likely to spend at least ten or fifteen relatively uninterrupted minutes with him, such as at a party, a potluck social after church, or an airport bar. Bring the conversation to a temporary or permanent end by going to the restroom or checking your watch and blurting, "My plane is leaving!" When you walk away, consider the following questions:

- What do you know about this man?
- What does he know about you?
- How do you feel when you walk away? If you were talked *at,* you may feel wonderful when you're with him but get the feeling something's missing when you walk away.
- Did he seem to spend a lot of time remembering descriptions or ideas of things in his own life?

In Chapter 5, when I teach you how to baseline in preparation to spot a lie, I will give you basics of reading eye movement. After you've read that chapter, repeat this exercise with this added element of observation: Watch what his eyes do when he talks. If they signal that he is recalling events, it's possible that he's doing very little listening to you, but a lot of listening to his inner storyteller.

safe to say that most men in this society now understand we need to bait you into our cave rather than drag you there. We have developed complex strategies to convey our masculinity—some manifestations being so bizarre that only a man could think of them.

Generally, men swagger and stand stronger, rather than fuss with their hair and take time out to look in the mirror, when they ruffle their plumage for a woman. That is, of course, unless the man is metrosexual. You will find plenty of heterosexual men who preen like meticulous women, primarily in urban environments around the world.

Somewhere in the middle, between the heterosexual man who grooms excessively with feminine standards and the complete slob of maleness, is the average man. This is the man who bathes, brushes his teeth, and keeps his nails trimmed and his shoes clean. And that's just about it. When he ruffles his plumage, he might try to look more muscular by wearing a shirt that's tight at his arms or look more *au currant* by wearing the latest cool shirt. He will not, however, be so hyper-concerned about appearance that he will appear feminine.

You should note, however, that men do many things to attract women: clothing choice, hobbies, just about anything you can think of can be derived from a man's desire to attract women. Raucous behavior in a bar stands out as one of the most common, as in, "Watch me sink that ball in the corner pocket" said so loudly that you can hear it four blocks away. I have known men who have taken up everything short of quilting because there are lots of women involved in a particular hobby. These men have no idea what attracts women and move from fad to fad trying to get some female attention. I told an acquaintance years ago why I wouldn't go antiquing with him to find women: "They hang out at the gynecologist's office, too, but I'm not going there, either."

Most heterosexual men instinctively know that movement in the shoulders, not the hips, makes them look masculine. Conversely, most gay men know that hip action emphasizes the feminine. Some men just do not seem to have the right instincts, though, and the result is laughable incongruity when one of those confused men ruffles his plumage.

I have seen many guys who are so worried about appearing manly that they invest in cowboy boots that will never go with ten miles of horse manure. Another common deception is biker gear. Strip the leather and do-rags off of some of these guys and they are weak and mushy, with flabby old-lady arms. A real biker doesn't care you if you like him or his outfit; a poser cares about both.

In other communities, it's the amount of physical risk that defines masculinity. Men try to fit the profile of a man with lots of testosterone—James Bond, for example—and if they're lucky, wind up with only reparable injuries until they mature.

I spent my life in the Army, arguably the most testosterone-filled environment there is. When we men are left to our own devices in that setting, we are incorrigible. We go after too much of everything: sex, food, alcohol, violence. What I found is that most of the tough guys were either secretly in love with a woman who does not exist—an archetype—or in love with one they could not have. Men who live in the most masculine of worlds are often not exposed regularly to feminine behaviors and do not communicate well with women. That creates a new dynamic for them.

EXERCISE 10. PLUMAGE RUFFLING

OBJECTIVE: Focus on what men do when they want to impress a woman.

This is definitely more fun with friends. Watch and experience the male trying to be all that he can be. Pick out men of different stature and physical appeal, which can have more to do with grooming and presence than features.

In this exercise, take note of what men do even when they aren't interacting with a woman. They might be standing in line for a hot dog or talking with a bartender, but you will know if they are merely standing in line, or standing in line while trying to look sexy, because of the signals.

These signals may vary a bit depending on whether you are in the midst of a political crowd in Washington, D.C., or a country bar in Texas, but they will all shake out into two, basic categories: posturing and hyperbole. Posturing means taking a stance intended to project a certain image. Hyperbole means that the attitude—of masculinity or compassion, for example—is amplified.

Here are some things to watch for—and a couple of them may not even be intentional moves on his part:

- Hands on the hips with fingers pointing toward genitals
- Wearing boots or shoes to make him taller than normal; boots particularly throw the weight forward to help project a masculine stance
- Wearing clothes and using his arms to convey a broad-shouldered body
- Using verbal plumage, either to sound more masculine ("I killed nine men with an eyelash") or in the form of self-deprecating humor ("My nuts are the size of filberts")

Ask yourself what you want—not what *they* want. Do you want a man who acts like a man in the Army definition? Or a man who acts like a man on the runway in Paris or Milan? Or a man who walks his dog every day at dawn because that's what his dog likes? They are not mutually exclusive, by the way, and whether they are the same man or different, they may ruffle their plumage in different ways.

Think of things a man has done to attract you. What were the physical things? Did he use a prop? (Think "puppy on a leash.") Intellectual? Intangible? Overlook nothing.

Just like monkeys, birds, and males throughout the animal kingdom, men strut, preen, fluff, bow, and inflate to make ourselves look sexier than we look normally. Sometimes, human males have the presence of mind to do it in a way that lets a particular female know that he's doing it for her. For example, a man who notices you at a conference reception overhears you order a glass of cabernet sauvignon from the bartender, instead of just "red wine." He might ruffle his plumage for you by talking about his collection of rare "cabs."

Noticing ways that men try to catch your attention can help you whether or not the guy is comfortable in his own skin. Externals like clothing will tell you a lot, just as they do with women. Take a look at women who have a lot going for them but who may be uncomfortable about their weight, for example. They are often perfectly manicured, and they select accessories like their jewelry and scarves carefully. Whether it's men or women who are uncomfortable in their skin, if they have any self-respect, they do something to distract you from the "bad" and focus on the good.

That's the positive view. And then there's the less than positive. I once knew a young man who wore a kilt around a small Georgia town because "it was him." That might be normal in a heavily Scottish community, but in little Georgia towns, that's just plain weird. Do you think he was comfortable being *him*? No.

Men who see themselves as less-than often do something pecu-
liar to get your attention, and that is why this particular guy wore
a kilt.

Positive or Negative

Some professions require a person to be default negative,
that is, to look at a situation with one question at the forefront:
"What's wrong?" Auditors, doctors, plumbers, lawyers, police
officers, investigative journalists—anybody society counts on to
fix things—have to approach new situations with that kind of
critical eye. On the other hand, people in public relations, fund-
raising, and kindergarten classrooms tend to be default-positive
types. They look at the good news and promote the positive story.
Both types can work well together. In fact, they should be paired
in many circumstances because their points of view are comple-
mentary. That doesn't mean they necessarily make good partners
in a personal relationship; it all depends on a couple of factors.
How well you get along with someone who's different from you
depends on how extreme that person is in representing the positive or negative, as well as on how tolerant you are. You don't
want to date someone who will make you miserable by criticizing
the food at every restaurant, the acting in every movie, and your
friends' taste in furniture. And if you tend toward the skeptical/
critical side, a guy who thinks that you can cure AIDS with nice
music and lollipops will probably make you nuts.

If you're a default-positive person, rank how much these habits that suggest a default-negative personality bother you. Use a

scale of 1 to 5, with 5 meaning that it makes you want to smack a guy who does the following:

- Salts his food before he tastes it
- Refuses to see a movie on the basis of a title, before knowing anything about it
- Complains without knowing if there's a basis for a complaint, usually beginning with "if," as in, "If this drink is watery . . ." or "If that guy even thinks about changing the channel on the TV. . ."

What's the commonality here? The unhealthy default-negative types look for a problem before they even know what's going on. They focus on a problem, rather than a solution, whereas the healthy default-negative person will *spot* the problem and then *pursue* a solution.

If you're a default-negative person, rank how much these default-positive personality traits bother you, on a scale of 1 to 5:

- Compliments the server on the food even before he tastes it
- Enthusiastically agrees to go somewhere or to do something without knowing a bit about the activity being proposed
- Figures that people will be thoughtful enough not to smoke around you, even though smoking is permitted where you are

What's the commonality here? The unhealthy default-positive types assume everything's fine before they even know what's going on. Without even evaluating the circumstance, they declare "everything's good," whereas the healthy default-positive person will be open-minded and optimistic without being a sucker.

Self-Perception

In general, men and women view their physical appearances differently. In a 2004 study entitled "The Real Truth About Beauty: A Global Report," only 2 percent of the 3,200 women interviewed considered themselves beautiful. You might be one of those many women for whom "beautiful" is an extreme term, but consider what else this team led by Dr. Nancy Etcoff of Harvard University found: Only 9 percent of the women described themselves as "attractive." "Good-looking" and "cute" were in a dead heat at 7 percent.

The remaining 82 percent of women studied thought of themselves in mundane terms like "normal" or "average." You can bet that if men were the subjects of the same study, the numbers on the "handsome" end would be much higher.

Two factors enter the equation from men's point of view. First, we rarely discuss the subject of our looks. Also, we do not readily talk about how good-looking another man is.

In short, the pressure is not there to evaluate or classify our looks as much as it is for a woman. A man will generally measure self-worth on other scales: physical strength, intelligence, competence, the ability to provide, and so on.

A man might think a great deal of himself because he knows he is a great guy. There is nothing wrong with that kind of self-respect because it reflects a reasonable self-assessment as opposed to a comparison to another guy, or to you. Some substantial egos are well founded in competence, good looks, genius, or a number of other factors that place the guy out of the norm. Well-founded egos take shape in a person who is comfortable in his skin, with no need to demonstrate how much better he is than you or anyone else. Men in this category sometimes use self-deprecating humor to try to make other people feel better about being around them. For many of the "sexiest men alive," it's part of their charm.

Men who think a little too much of themselves are usually normal guys with inflated egos; Momma or Daddy may have spent too many hours praising and coddling him. They come in lots of flavors, depending on whether or not they are strong, well educated, rich, tough, and so on. Most of their gimmicks are either mildly amusing or mildly annoying. Some men strut like roosters or tell you how much more they make than the next guy; others use sarcasm and wit to show you how bright they are.

EXERCISE 11. THE MIRROR

OBJECTIVE: Take a close look at how you perceive yourself.

Make a list of the things about you that you are quietly (or not so quietly) proud of. For the externals, consider face, body, hair, clothes, accessories, fingernails—everything on the surface. For the internals, consider brains, kindness, spirituality, hospitality, and other qualities, talents, and attributes that no one would know about unless you demonstrated them. As you go down the list, make notes on how you accept and acknowledge compliments about these attributes. When you get a compliment about your beauty, for example, do you say, "Well, I guess my parents had good taste in mates"? Or do you give a straightforward "Thank you"?

When a man uses self-deprecating humor in a sarcastic fashion, it is usually indicative of a super-sized ego. For instance, let's say I meet a really handsome actor and he says, "Well, we can't all be as gorgeous as you are, Mr. Hartley." That would be the kind of sarcastic self-deprecation that is not charming, but it's not necessarily ingratiating, either. Bright people do this often and think nothing of it. This is an ego you may find amusing until you are on the receiving end of its attack. You don't have to put up with their quirks if you set them straight when you first meet them. Just reinforce the communication you like by listening and questioning and go to the ladies' room when they wander off into ego-land.

And then there are the men who engage in self-aggrandizing behavior because of insecurities. They might be slight or profound, with over-compensating behavior ranging from bragging about their high school football days to full-blown narcissism, which I cover in Chapter 11.

EXERCISE 12. THE CAMERA

OBJECTIVE: Gain insight into how he perceives himself.

Watch how the man you're observing responds to compliments. Does he quietly acknowledge them? Come back with self-deprecating humor? Get sarcastic, as though you don't know what you're talking about? Aggrandize the quality? ("And you should see my biceps, too!) The response is an indicator of his comfort level within his skin.

The more normal of the men in this group constantly tell you about their IQ, shoe size, income, or how much they can bench press because they need approval; they are fragile. A man like this limits your options to approving or being removed from his circle. One of the best ways to determine how a man perceives himself is to watch his interaction with others (*see Exercise 12 on previous page*).

Conflict Style

Stress styles vary from person to person. The kindest and gentlest people can turn into ogres with the right stimulus *if* they have a stress style that tends toward controlling: They lose control over a situation, and they go straight to an emotional state. And then there are people who get stressed out over little things, but in a crisis, their logic and skills override an emotional response—two different styles in the same person, depending on the situation.

As we go through life, we should wake up to what stress styles are acceptable and what behaviors make things better, not worse. If my experience is that every time things go wrong, I step in, take control of the situations, and fix them, then guess what my stress style will be when something goes wrong in my life? This is the stereotype of the oldest child, by the way.

This is important to discover early because your Prince Charming may have a stress style that differs dramatically from his business-as-usual demeanor.

Consider the following stress-style indicators, which you may observe or find out by talking to people who know him. How does he deal with work-related issues? Is he even-tempered, a "nice guy" to the end who listens? Does he cut people off in mid-sentence, jumping to an offensive posture quickly? Or is he somewhere in between? His behavior in a work situation will suggest how he acts when he's in an environment without the restraint of others' expectations of a professional demeanor. Learned behaviors that work are hard to jettison; it's unlikely (but not impossible) that he's thoroughly wonderful during stressful times at work but a raging fool at home.

When things do not go his way, how does he react? Does he wrest control from other people, or does he try to make things the way he would like by tactfully influencing others' behavior?

Manners

Real manners have two facets: socially acceptable behavior and genuine behavior. A man who treats you "right," and then insults a waitress for dropping his toast on the floor, is a man who knows how to treat you "wrong."

A man with bad manners in the social sense may still be a well-mannered individual. He's the guy who hasn't had the exposure to socially acceptable ways of doing things—he picks up the wrong fork at dinner—but he displays courteous behavior to everyone from the guy who changes his oil to the surgeon removing his gall bladder. You can train a guy to use the right fork, but do not hold any hope of remolding a rude man.

I can wrap up a lot of what is covered in this chapter by talking about manners. A well-bred man (translation: a man who is trained to do the right thing) can present a great first impres-

sion, but get him in a slightly stressful situation and your second
impression might not be so good. Or get him talking about himself, and you may realize that his breeding is only skin deep.

With this in mind, do you think that the man, or men, you
observed in the exercises in this chapter might have fooled you?
Do you think you drew any naïve conclusions based on manners?
If so, go back and do the exercises again with a fresh perspective
before you move on to active observation.

5.

Observe:
Stage One Contact

If you have ever watched a cop show with good interrogation scenes, such as *The Closer*, then you know the detective does not rely wholly on what the person offers. Deputy Police Chief Brenda Johnson (Kyra Sedgwick) solicits certain responses to get behaviors she wants. It's now time for you to model her, to move from being a passive observer to someone who causes some of the interaction.

When I interrogate, I can watch all day in the nonintrusive style of primatologist Jane Goodall. But without introducing some element of control into the situation, I still have no idea whether or not I'm looking at the "right" person. Now you get to create circumstances in which you actively engage your man of interest so you can learn specific things. You won't just watch him dance; you will pick the music and dance with him. It's the stimulus-response approach to discovering a guy's habits and true nature.

This kind of active observation involves myriad activities. Some relate to early encounters, maybe even before an actual date; I call that "stage one contact." Others can only occur after you've gotten to know someone; I'll cover those later.

In this chapter, I'll give you the tools to answer these questions up front:

- Is he attracted to you?
- Is he lying to you? Of course he is, but is it good lying ("Yeah, I love cats") or bad lying ("I'm not married")?
- How much control does he have (or want to have) over the conversation?
- What's the best way to build rapport with him?
- How do you maintain a certain amount of healthy tension? You do not want the guy you want to slip into a default "let's be friends" because things get a little too comfortable.

Baselining

A polygraph, the device most people call a lie detector, is named from Greek roots meaning "many lines." The polygraph is just that: a chart with multiple lines that map blood pressure, heart rate, and other physiological variables. When something on one of the graphs changes, it's a visual alarm. But besides an outright lie, things like idiosyncratic twitches and an overdose of caffeine can also make the graphs go a little haywire.

What does a polygraph expert do to sort the lies from the glitches? He *baselines* to find out what is normal for the subject in a low-stress environment by asking him questions such as "What's your middle name?" and "Where did you go to high school?" The machine then looks for deviations from the baseline to spot a lie. I use the term *baseline* to mean basically the same concept, but without relying on a machine. The baselining I'm teaching you is your portable polygraph that will help you detect changes in body language and tone of voice that usually go with telling a lie, even a "white" lie.

You began to answer the question "What's normal for him?" in Chapter 4. When you baseline a man, you start from this low-key beginning and look for deviations that indicate something has changed in that odd brain of his. When the brain changes, the body follows. Even the most polished individuals have difficulty disconnecting the two. Some behaviors indicate sexual tension; others show that he really does not like your cat. Getting a good baseline will help you know the difference.

Baselining Basics

Eye movement, cadence and tone of voice, gestures, and even word choices constitute key elements of your baseline. It might be perfectly normal for you to blink a lot, speak rapidly, or flail your arms when you talk. When you deviate from that, there's a reason: stress. You might feel "good stress," like sexual attraction to a guy, or the kind of "bad stress" related to telling a lie, tripping down the stairs, or not knowing the right fork to use at a formal dinner party.

To baseline a guy, start by looking at the gestures you already know: illustrators, barriers, regulators, and adaptors. Does he usually touch his nose a lot? Does he always have a higher-than-average blink rate? Is tapping and drumming nothing more than a frequent reminder of his high energy? Look for everything from head to toe to get a clear sense for what is normal for him when he is relaxed.

Keep these signs in mind as I give you prime indicators of stress, and then complete Exercise 13 to nail the skill set.

Cadence

I define cadence as the speed at which something moves along. That can be the rate of a man's speech, how quickly his expressions change, and even the rate at which he gestures. All of these give you a feel for who a person is. When you learn what is normal cadence for him, you will automatically notice when cadence changes.

Tone

Every person has heard, "It's not what you said, it's how you said it!" Everyone has a normal tone for conversation; most of us have different tones for family and friends, acquaintances, and superiors. That tone difference can be a good indicator of sexual intent as well.

Diction

While it's true that most of what we say is not in the words, but rather in the delivery, that still doesn't render the words themselves insignificant. Word choice gives you major clues about what message the person is trying to deliver. In this first step of baselining, as you watch your subject, note his choice of words. Is he the evening news anchor? Pop culture boy? This baseline will come into play when you start to get to know the real person.

EXERCISE 13. NORMAL FOR HER/HIM

OBJECTIVE: Get to know a couple of friends better through their idiosyncrasies and deviations from their baselines.

The next time you're just hanging out with friends, pay attention to how they normally talk and move:

- Pace of speech: Fast, medium, slow
- Tone: Excited/dramatic, even/calm, expressionless
- Word choices: Slangy/street talk, average vocabulary, academic
- Overall movement: Fidgety, fluid, restrained

Next, bring up a touchy topic. Open your eyes to the differences in behavior from the relaxed and fun atmosphere to a situation in which passions or tension rise. Make a mental note of how the pace of speech, tone, word choices, and overall movement of your friends change.

Baseline for Attraction

A contrived situation skews a baseline. Because many first encounters and first dates with guys qualify as contrived situations, you need to do your baseline in two stages: first, determine whether or not he is attracted to you, and second, ascertain whether or not he is lying to you.

As I said in the introduction, the manufactured nature of the encounter is one clear thing that dating has in common with interrogation. It causes huge apprehension about how the other person in the encounter—interrogator or potential mate—will perceive you. When a source enters an interrogation room and all he sees is a bright light, single chair, and a table, he automatically forms expectations about what will happen next. Stress may build quickly, or it may remain at a low level, depending on his experience with similar situations.

Blind dates can feel like interrogations of the worst sort. The only thing the two people involved may have in common is a friend who has no idea what either person desires.

Depending on past experience, a date you've both agreed to in advance is not much different. You engage a man in conversation in what he (and you) may perceive as strained and artificial circumstances. The more experience both of you have in the dating scene, the more likely you are to behave in a relaxed, normal way with each other. The less experience and/or the greater your interest in the other person, the more likely you and he are to show your apprehension. He will have glitchy behavior, and so will you.

If the guy finds you attractive, he will give you vocal and verbal signals:

- He will shift to a softer, slower type of speech than he would use in the office or while chatting with his buddies.
  - Does his cadence slow, or conversely, does he suddenly shift into a higher gear as he makes jokes?
  - Here's a place to use projection: If you slow your cadence, does he mirror that change? Good for you: That is a sign of attraction. As a man starts to mirror female behavior, he will get softer. That doesn't mean his personality is changing. His blocky, masculine behavior will just automatically start to fade as he softens in mirroring someone he is attracted to.

- His tone of voice will change. Maybe he'll go over the top because that's how he responds to nervous tension, or he will soften noticeably. While softening is a good sign that he is moving to a more emotional state, the opposite is not necessarily a bad sign. The reality may be that he is just nervous that he might mess up a good thing. (In Chapter 6, I will help you to expand the skill set to determine the source of his tension.)

- His word choice will move from masculine to what he perceives as feminine or sensitive, or he will go to the opposite end of his vocabulary and use hyper-masculine words. Either extreme at inappropriate times is a bad sign.

- Pay attention to any change in his use of illustrators, barriers, adaptors, regulators, and proximity.

  - Does he drop a barrier, such as move his latté to the side instead of holding it in front of him while he talks? Playing with the beer bottle can have a dual meaning: When he moves it in front of him, it's a barrier. When he peels the label, he using an adaptor.

  - Does he maintain prolonged eye contact? Not the creepy kind, the interested kind. If he is practicing his hypnosis act, then practice your disappearing act.

  - Does he fidget, that is, use an adaptor to release nervous energy and try to get more comfortable with you? That is normal, especially for a younger guy. The more comfortable he gets over time, the less he will fidget.

  - Does he ruffle his plumage, either physically by squaring his posture or intellectually by ramping up the wit?

Depending on whether or not he sees himself as physical, he may use one or both.

- Does he make an attempt to stand closer to you?
- Does he begin tilting his head and softening, matching
your moves as he does in three-quarter cadence?

Humans are relatively primitive creatures. Although our brains
have evolved with a frontal cortex for higher thought, it is our
primal system that prepares us for sexual activity. Think "fight or
flight" in reverse. "Fight or flight" takes blood away from repro-
ductive systems and sends it to muscles needed to protect life
and limb. But in the heat of sexual attraction, the system floods
the genitals with blood flow for erections, lubrication, and other
functions linked to the propagation of the species. The blood flow
engorges mucosa—not only the genital areas, but also eye lids
and lips, to name two obvious places. The result: bedroom eyes
and pillow lips. It is why women pay for collagen injections so
their lips look like Angelina Jolie's. Full lips broadcast the signal
"I'm ready for sex." You can see the same signs in a man, too.

Baseline for Lies

When you walk into a venue where flirtatious conversation might
occur—bar, office, church, gym—you need to be prepared to
sort truth from fiction. How are you going to go about doing
that? You could lug around a polygraph machine and play Jack
Byrnes, connecting some poor Fokker to it at every party you

go to á la *Meet the Parents*. Or you could activate the machine between your ears, which actually gives you better information when used properly.

I will take you through a condensed head-to-toe analysis of what signs suggest that the guy might be lying to you. Keep in the mind that lies come in four different flavors, even though the signs of their use can be the same:

OMISSION: He leaves out pertinent information in an attempt to construct a true statement. You ask, "What happened at the party after I left?" He answers, "I had one more beer, and then went home." He omits the fact that he went home the next morning.

COMMISSION: He makes something up. You ask, "What happened at the party after I left?" He answers, "I got a splitting headache and went home right away."

EMBELLISHMENT: He adds a few decorations to the truth. You ask, "What happened at the party after I left?" He answers, "I had another beer, which put me a little over the edge, so I found a quiet corner and took a nap while things kept going, and then I felt well enough to drive myself home."

TRANSFERENCE: This simply means taking a slice of someone else's truth and making it your own. You ask, "What happened at the party after I left?" He says, "John got wasted so I drove him home." It's a tough lie to defend because you're pulling a story out of context.

Eyes

The illustration below will guide you in learning four things about reading eye movement to determine whether or not someone might be lying. You'll find out where a person looks when he's doing any of the following:

1. Remembering an image or sound
2. Creating an image or sound
3. Experiencing deep emotion
4. Analyzing or calculating

The absence of irises in the faces below allows you to learn to baseline eye movement by asking a person questions, and then drawing in the dark spots for yourself. Practice on your girlfriends so that you don't need the drawing when you do it with your date! Oh, and be subtle when you ask the questions, or he *will* think he's in an interrogation.

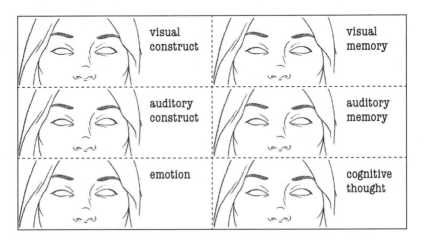

EXERCISE 14. BASELINING EYE MOVEMENT

OBJECTIVE: Find out where your guy looks when he's remembering versus making something up.

Asking very basic questions will elicit eye movement associated with remembering an image or imagining a sound. You need to ask questions he will not, or cannot, lie to you about because there's a high likelihood you know the answers. That is called a control question in interrogator-speak. These questions need to be simple, but not too simple. The questions should use memories only from one sense, such as song lyrics or driving directions. Here are a few examples of control questions:

Visual recall: "How do I get to Murphy's Pub from here?" or "If I'm at Times Square, how do I get to the Empire State Building?"

Auditory recall: "What is the seventh word of the *Star Spangled Banner*?" or "How does that song from the new James Bond movie begin?"

Did his eyes move up and to his left, or up and to his right when you asked him the visual questions? Did his eyes move toward his left ear, or toward his right ear when you asked him to remember sounds? Now you know which direction he moves his eyes when he's recalling something. When they move to the other side, he's making it up.

The eye movement for calculation, or cognitive thought, is the same for nearly everyone: down and to the person's left. If you are trying to do mental arithmetic to figure out your waiter's tip, for example, it's likely you'll glance down left.

The eye movement for emotion is down and to the person's right. Watch people at a funeral or any other situation involving intense emotion. You may see just their eyes cast downward, but you may also see the entire head leaning down right.

Body

If you see a man's eyes move in a direction that indicates he's creating—a nice way of saying "deceiving"—then watch for adaptors. Leg rubbing, hand wringing, finger tapping, neck clenching, or other signs of stress that occur along with the deviations in eye movement should raise your suspicions. I'm not saying you've definitely nabbed a liar. I am saying you have detected two indicators that something might be off.

I mentioned earlier that a man might start off his encounter with you more fidgety than normal, and then slow down as he becomes more comfortable. The inverse can happen, too, and that may be a bad sign. Let's say his norm is hyper-boy, someone whose baseline is high energy and constant movement. He suddenly stops this adaptive behavior when you begin discussing a certain touchy topic. One reason could be that he is diverting energy to his brain and engaging his imagination to answer your question. Look for other indicators of deception.

Taking Control

You need to know how a man you find attractive takes control of a conversation or situation—or if he's utterly incapable of doing that. Start by figuring out how *you* take control of a conversation. What can your personality handle? What is your natural style—overt or subtle? After that, you'll be in a good position to consider the other person's style, and you will see how your style may change in response to his behavior.

Consider for a moment that you wanted to talk about ritual practices that subjugate women. What is the *most comfortable* way for you to take the conversation to that topic?

Option #1: Lateral Conversation

Examples of this tactic include analogy and metaphor to slide the conversation in a different direction. Most of the time, this lateral conversation is intended to cause someone to think of a topic that you want to cover. You manipulate them into changing the subject for you. You control the conversation, but the other person feels as though it is her idea. This is an art that some people master with practice and others do well naturally. Note in the following conversation how you could quickly go from an inconsequential remark to a contentious topic, which leads into the subject you want to discuss.

YOU: There's nothing good on TV.

HER: Every once in a while there's something decent on.

YOU: Mostly on the premium channels, like HBO, and—oh, where did I see that? The other day there was this really good special on Darfur.

HER: Yeah, that is a real tragedy what's going on. We should do something about it.

YOU: A lot of people have tried, but there are just things you can't change. Even when people from other places come here, some of the same nasty things happen. There was a piece on the Atlanta news about a couple from sub-Saharan

Africa. The wife turned her husband in for carrying out
this horrible tradition on their daughter—

HER: Omigod! I saw that story!

Now the topic is open for discussion. You've just gone from
"There's nothing good on TV" to the subject of a brutal ritual
practice designed to subjugate women.

Option #2: The Direct Approach

The alternative is taking the as-the-crow-flies approach to the
topic. There's nothing oblique about this tactic.

HER: We need to respect traditions of people in other parts of
the world.

YOU: Even if it means that a girl's father gets to decide whether
she goes to school, marries a man old enough to be her grand-
father, or is ever physically capable of having an orgasm?

EXERCISE 15. CHANGE THE SUBJECT

OBJECTIVE: Determine your natural style of taking control.

Do this experiment with a girlfriend, but do not tell her beforehand what
you're trying to do. Just get her opinion after the fact. Talk about something
that's likely to arouse strong feelings, such as sex, politics, or religion. Try to
steer the conversation toward a specific aspect of the topic that would be
odd for both of you to discuss.

A man who is attracted to you might completely reverse his normal tendency toward either lateral conversation or the direct approach. He might be a direct guy who feels that he'll turn you off, so he modifies his style. Or he might be a lateral guy who thinks you won't see him as manly unless he asserts himself. If you want to move him toward his natural style, steer the conversation toward a hot topic, just as you did in the exercise with your friend.

Establish Rapport

In an interrogation, rapport building can be positive, neutral, or negative. In a dating situation, you will encounter analogous conditions to these interrogations, and you could think of them as falling somewhere on a continuum between "the neg" (to borrow the shorthand term for *negative* that Neil Strauss used in *The Game*) and "I'll do anything for you." Most likely, when you establish rapport, you take an approach that falls somewhere in the middle.

The Negative Tactic

The negative tactic involves challenges or even insults that serve as an invitation: You use them because you want the person to struggle to get close to you. He has to show his value before you go any further. Be aware of the reasons he might do this to you right after he meets you. Maybe he bleeds a little nervousness through a playful, negative rapport. Then again, maybe he's truly mean-spirited or manipulative. Many women are drawn to bad boys, and this is what bad boys do; they are the unbroken horses that women see as arousing challenges. You need to keep aware of whether you are making a choice or are going with your default reaction.

An example of a healthy negative tactic is two quick-witted people who relish sarcasm but do not aim it at each other. When a woman friend of mine—a former bodybuilder—first met a professional comedian who was six-foot-four and beautifully built, she called him a wimp and literally picked him up. Hoisted above the crowd, he made a crack about her display of muscle. She retorted that if he'd had any, he would not have let her do it. They slung barbs at each other until they ended up in bed, and then in a long-term, great relationship.

An unhealthy negative rapport builds from an insult that really is an insult. Maybe he's an athlete who says to you, "You obviously wouldn't understand how much it means to me to work out every day."

A person may simply criticize something obvious to get you to disclose something more intimate or protected as you defy his criticism of you. It is one of the best ploys in the intelligence-collecting arsenal.

The Positive Tactic

The positive tactic puts you in the role of nice person, complimenting him and showing interest in what he says. Turn this around in an extreme variation. Let's say a guy begins his conversation with you in a friendly way and keeps getting warmer, and sweeter, and gentler. Go to the ladies' room to cool off and ask yourself: Is he desperate? If you conclude "yes," that's no reason to discard him, but it's a big reason to make sure you do not go home with him that night. Whether he's desperate for love, sex, or both, he's still desperate.

An example of a truly positive tactic is listening to someone talk about her tough day and then responding appropriately: supportive, but not foolish; incisive without being judgmental.

The negative side of positive is either the manipulator or the toady. If this is you, you need to stop it. If this is him, here's the program. The toady will kiss your ass because it's your ass. You can cut him a break because he's nervous or realize that he has a major self-esteem problem. The manipulator is a user. You use your intuition. Leave now.

Last and most definitely least, the neutral tactic is something you will want to use if you don't have a strong interest in or feeling for him, one way or the other. You are building rapport in the context of an average conversation.

Rapport in Dating

Most people think of a date as an exercise in building positive rapport. But a lot of odd negative behavior comes with the territory because, first and foremost, men who are interested in you operate with the thought, "I want to impress you so that you come back for more." That is why I have heard so many guys say stupid things like, "Nice guys finish last," or "Women like assholes." They often interpret the fact that you do not want to date weak and mindless men in crude terms.

EXERCISE 16. NICE OR NEG

OBJECTIVE: Know whether a positive come-on or a negative one is more likely to trigger rapport with you.

Find a guy you do not already know at work, in class, at a football game, or wherever this kind of appealing guy might be. Talk with him for a few minutes, or as much time as it takes to establish minimal rapport. Now make a list of things that attract you to that particular person. Or if talking with him made you really dislike him, make notes on that, too.

- How did his style of establishing rapport either reinforce your attraction to him or repel you?
- If it reinforced your attraction, merge your before and after lists, and then organize the appealing qualities in order of importance.
- What did you learn about what works with you—nice or neg?

The magic is for men to understand how to be perceived as strong while not acting arrogant. Remember, we males often fall short in the subtlety department; you will see extremes as we try to impress you.

Positive rapport is nothing more than complimenting you, a man's way of conveying overtly that he likes you. Guys can get stupid with it, so if you really like a man but wish he would be a little less Mr. Rogers, just let him know. He may be so smitten that he can't measure how far off the mark he is. At the extreme end is the icky sweet, he-likes-everything-you-like loser with no personality of his own. If you want that kind of positive rapport, get a dog.

Negative rapport can be a guy's natural response to making people like him more. It is the equivalent to horsing around in the locker room, snapping each other on the butt with towels.

Guys like this may assume the same kind of behavior will make you notice how manly they are. There are the insidious ones who say negative things because they know some women will be drawn to punishment. These women need to be made wrong; they want abuse. You are not one of them, so stay away from guys like that.

Sexual Rapport-Building

In rapport-building, some kinds of tension are desirable.

I have male friends who always end up falling into the role of "friend" with women. Recently I have seen more and more women on television shows complaining about the analogous thing. So how do you prevent that friendly, zero-sexual-tension outcome?

As you start to build rapport, act like the relationship is meant to go somewhere. Be honest: Neither of you wants to end up with nothing more than a friend with special privileges. You may get there, but that is not the ideal you had in mind. Most people find it difficult to cross that barrier of "just friends" once it is established.

Men commonly stray into the gray area of friends-with-an-attraction because they start the relationship as an acquaintance or friend and then suddenly see what other men see in her. They find it easy to fall in love with a person they already know and respect who, perhaps much to their surprise, is also a woman. The woman thinks, "What's this about, good buddy?" and that ends that.

If you want a relationship to involve romance, start and maintain a flirtatious relationship from the beginning. If you see yourself becoming one of the guys, set boundaries. You might become his favorite "one of the guys" because of your optional sports package, but that is likely all.

You want tension. You want that constant feeling of never becoming too familiar prior to your first sexual contact. If he knows everything about you and has never slept with you, what is going to change after sex? How can the relationship go to breathtaking heights?

Rapport Means Results

In the interrogation world, my first contact with a guy involves figuring out who he is and where he fits into my agenda. I start by bringing him into a room and establishing some basics about his personality, priorities, and habits. Along the way, I maintain an aura of power and mystery about who I am and what I am about. After that, I design interactions with him that allow me to probe who he really is.

The dance of his reacting to my cues and my responding to what he says starts a process that determines whether or not this is the right guy *and* whether or not I can get him to do what I want. If I find he's exactly the right guy to talk with, and I think we can come to an agreement on what he needs to do to help me, then my next step is motivating behavior. I get him to do what I want him to do because we have a solid rapport. Good relationships start the same way, but not necessarily with all that drama.

You have gotten to a point that determined your criteria for someone you want to date, narrowed groups, and started to understand who he is and what he wants. You are now well along the way to proceeding to a deal. Maybe.

Can the guy you've picked out provide what you are looking for? Can you come to a compromise about how to get it? If you answered, "I think so," then you are ready for the next steps.

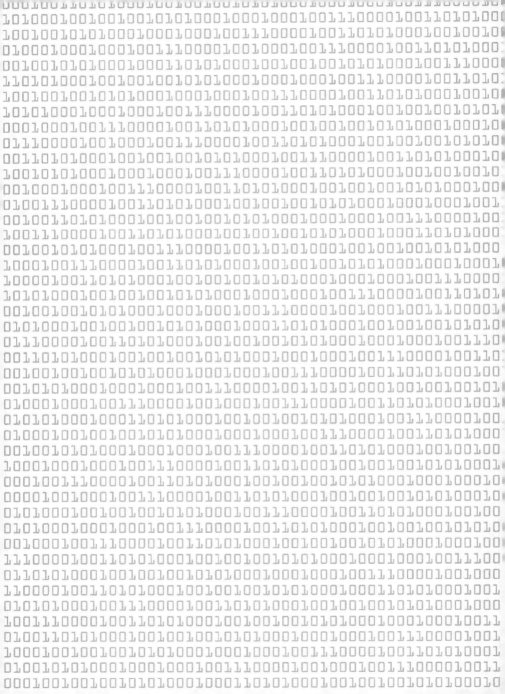

6.

Observe:
Stage Two Contact

During interrogations, bad guys are often capable of collaborating with each other effectively. Some will try to trick me into thinking they know more than they do to take the heat off the truly valuable guy. One might project that he's a chemical weapons genius who can't take the heat, while the other makes like a thug who says he knows everything and doesn't know anything. Meanwhile, my preoccupation with them is designed to divert attention from the military strategist sitting in the corner.

When I interrogate, there are the initial impressions I have based on observation prior to and during initial contact, and then the impressions I have after forcing a source into a psychologically uncomfortable situation. After that, I can notice the real tells (to put it in poker terms) that a guy leaks when I have him on the run.

My tools for discerning the difference are skills like baselining, which is vital in terms of understanding what kind of person I am dealing with. It also helps to know how he stores and sorts information; for example, that he thinks sequentially rather than randomly. I then use some relatively sophisticated, yet straightforward tools, such as asking questions that take into account how his brain works to find out what I want to know. The real trick is to not reveal to him what I want to know in this process. If I'm curious about why there are foreigners in his unit, I do not want to say, "So, what about those three people traveling with you who aren't from this country?" If I do, he will suddenly know that information seems valuable to me.

That's like your saying to a fabulous guy you've just met, "So, how many times in the past three months have you used a condom?" I'm here to tell you how you can get the information without exposing yourself like that.

You've scanned his personality, habits, and quirks and think you want to move forward. Now, in order to dig more deeply, you need to understand how he communicates and when he deviates from his normal style of communicating. Is he the right guy, or just the guy who says the right things because he's picked up on your cues? Is he on the level with you or using "little lies" to get what he wants?

Question Artfully

Interrogators are taught to use interrogatives—who, what, when, where, why, and how—as part of the basic mechanics of our craft. In contrast to your situation in meeting people, an interrogator is out to get the most information in the shortest period of time. So in trying to pick up a woman, a man with junior-interrogator skills and no social acumen might pull out an arsenal of key questions and say any of these things:

- Hello, how are you?
- Who did you come here with?
- What do I need to do to get you to leave here with me tonight?

Have you heard this line of questioning before, or something close to it? Probably. A lot of men never become masters of collecting information and subtlety in conversation. They ask obvious questions, and they expect obvious answers.

And then there is default-negative guy, who always talks like the high school kid forced to job hunt by his parents. He assumes rejection. He approaches potential dates with such sad sack lines as, "I don't suppose you'd want to talk to a guy like me, would you?"

My aim is to make sure you do not mimic either of those styles. I want to move you closer to getting the truth about whether or not he's married, has only a one-night stand in mind, is a momma's boy, or has boyfriend potential—but in a way that's artful.

As you read this chapter (and later put the information to use), you should take into consideration the following basic truths:

- People compartmentalize information.
- Men and women commonly store information differently.
- Answering a question is a process affected by the person's perception of why you want the information.

- After you ask a question, how a person responds—man or woman—is tinctured by storage and questioning styles, perception of your intent, and desired outcome.

Sorting Information—Men *Versus* Women

Think about the last time you had a car accident. If you've never had one, then think about some other event that traumatized you in some way. Here's a contrast between how women and men, generally speaking, would remember an accident.

Women

The human impact of the accident dominates. As a woman, it's common for you to think in terms of how you felt or how an event affected you or other people. Few women will write the bare facts of what happened. So, your narrative might be: *"He rammed into the trunk of my car when the light changed. Surprised me so much I couldn't even scream. I looked at him and he seemed horrified— like he was in shock."* Most women include details that highlight the results of the incident and why it happened: "He said he didn't even see me. My car is red—how could he not see me?"

Men

Structurally, male and female brains are not exactly the same. In practical terms, then, a man will most likely perceive and mentally record the same accident differently from you. Men typically engage in a single-channel thought process, meaning logical recall, instead of recall tinged with how they felt at the time. On the other hand, women pull in different channels concurrently. That's because the female brain has a more robust nerve connection between left and right hemispheres. Therefore, his short narrative might be: *"The light turned green and I proceeded toward the intersection. The height of the bus I was driving put me well above her small car."*

Projecting Intent

When a police officer questions you about an accident, that trained professional will ask questions that attempt to structure the information in a particular way. You'll hear questions such as:

- Which direction were you traveling?
- What time of the day was it?
- Was the sun in your face?
- Did the sun impact your decision-making capability?

This kind of questioning limits your options on answering, mitigating the gender factor and going to the heart of the matter. It's the questioner's intent to find out how much of this accident was your fault.

"Was the sun in your face?" The construction of that question reflects exactly how the officer would get you to admit guilt. It's a *minimizing strategy* that interrogators use. The officer asks you the question so that you can lay blame on something else. You say, "Yes," and so you automatically have an opening to talk about the sun being at fault. You've heard this used in countless crime shows and movies. That's how the clever detective or prosecutor gets the criminal to confess. Questions like "Was the sun in your face" do not necessarily extract the truth, therefore. Assume for a moment you were at fault, but the sun was not blinding you. Would you take the question as an opening to avert a conclusion about your guilt? Human nature says, "Yes." Your answer might be a truthful: "The sun was in my face." And then you might think, "Sure, the sun impacted my decision-making. I was thinking about getting home in time to go for a run before it got dark, and that's why I was speeding." But all you say is, "Yes." The trap here is that you are still guilty, but you feel better about it.

You use the same setup, projecting the same intent to minimize guilt, by asking a guy, "Does it make your wife angry that you're on the road so much?" You've given the married road warrior a reason to feel less guilty about any infidelity if he says "yes" because, after all, his wife is just an angry woman. Or you start the conversation with a young soldier: "Why is it that I never meet single men? Are you married?" Not now, he isn't! He says, "No, I'm not," as he casually pats his chest. The movement looks genuine as though he's swearing, when in fact, he is testing to see if his wedding ring is still on the chain holding his dog tag.

Minimizing: An Aid to Questioning

The technique of minimizing is something you want to use deliberately, not inadvertently, such as in the "angry wife" question.

Minimizing takes two forms: You can tell him that, by comparison, what he did wasn't so bad. ("Okay, so you cheated on me . . . at least it wasn't with my sister.") Or you accuse him of something far worse than what you think he did, so he readily admits what he really did:

> **YOU:** Several people told me they saw you kissing Suzie at that party!
>
> **HIM:** Good grief, all I did was put my hand on her rear end. I'm sorry!

Interrogators often use minimizing to elicit the truth from sources, and so do detectives, criminal lawyers in a courtroom, and even doctors who suspect a patient is hiding something:

> **DOCTOR:** Well, at least you don't have a burning sensation with these symptoms.
>
> **PATIENT:** No, but I do have some itching.

EXERCISE 17. IT IS NOT SO BAD

OBJECTIVE: Experiment with minimizing to see how it gets people to admit things they otherwise would not.

Start a conversation with someone during which you tell her the "most embarrassing thing" you've ever done—something juicy. She will probably turn around and share an embarrassing moment, too. Even though her story will probably not be as outrageous as yours, you will still hear something a bit shocking, because your self-exposure minimizes the embarrassment she would normally feel telling it.

Good Questions and Bad Questions

Some types of questions confuse anyone, and we ask people to stay away from them in the interrogation room. That is primarily because interrogators are on a mission in which questions serve a life-and-death purpose. Your questioning style is less life-and-death oriented, so you have more flexibility in using various types of questions.

I will both explain why the following types of questions are not a good idea and give you positive uses for each.

Vague Questions

Some questions are so confusing that no one can possibly understand what you are asking. They are fuzzy and badly phrased. Interrogators need to be very specific. A vague question such as, "What did you think about that?" would never be asked in the interrogation room. We would ask something specific: "What did you think about your ex-wife running off with the chaplain?"

You can use vague questions deliberately, however, to diffuse suspicion or pressure around a topic. When things start to heat up, ask a question that forces a man to ask for clarification, and then follow that up with another vague question. You may look a bit ditzy, but you can redirect entire lines of conversation this way:

HIM: "John told me that he saw you at the Superstar Hotel last Saturday."
YOU: "Yeah, what's going on with that hotel?"

HIM: "Looks like it's become a kind of pick-up place."

YOU: "I heard it's a PIB hotel—People In Black. Did he mention the PIBs?"

Compound Questions

Asking a question that has multiple pieces also lacks specificity. Which part of the question do you want him to answer?

You ask, "On Friday night, do you want to go to the movie and see Cheryl?" He could give lots of responses:

"Yes, I want to go to the movie, but I hate Cheryl."

"Wow. I like Cheryl. Are you inviting her to the movie with us?"

"Which movie?"

"Who's Cheryl?"

Use this deliberately when you want to see how a man reacts to a confusing option. If he narrows the options, it can show healthy logic and/or a need to take control: "I'd love to see a movie with you on Friday. Do you see that also involving Cheryl?"

Negative Questions

"Are you not married?" He says, "No." What the heck does that tell you? Use this one when you want to hide the truth from yourself.

In other words, when you're in search of the truth, ask the straight question: "Are you married?" Avoid the use of confusing negatives.

Leading Questions

One of my favorite bad interrogation lines ever is a student interrogator's question: "Do you have any weapons at all?" The source obviously knows the "correct" answer is, "No." In fact, the correct answer is so obvious that one wonders why anyone would bother asking the question. Young women often ask a version of this one: "You're not married, are you?"

On the positive side, leading questions typically invite a "yes" or "no" response and can be perfect for changing the subject. For example, you've been talking about something a little uncomfortable and you glance at his arms and say, "Do you work out every day of the week?" You have now led him into a conversation that is all about how wonderful he is, rather than how much you disagree on an issue. Sometimes that's good, just to get some distance on the topic.

Interpreting Intent

In addition to the gender difference, the way a man answers your questions can be colored by why he thinks you are asking the question.

Ask a man you've just met if he's married, and he will assume you want to know because you are interested in him. Ask a man you've just met if he's available, and he will assume you want to sleep with him. Questions like these imply intent. If you get a strange reaction to what you think is an innocent get-to-know-you question, then he may have missed the mark on your reason for asking it.

EXERCISE 18. WHY DO YOU WANT TO KNOW

OBJECTIVE: Find out how your guy responds when your reason for asking a question isn't clear. Is he offensive, defensive, or pensive?

Ask him a complex question without including enough information for him to answer easily. Make it a question about a controversial topic, but leave out data and make the question feel like a setup. For example, "Do you think lesbian couples have a better case for adopting than gay male couples?"

Watch for signs of stress (adaptors, such as twitching and rubbing), defensive actions (barriers, such as putting an arm or a drink between you), and offensive actions (illustrators, such as batoning). Do his tone of voice and choice of words match his body language?

Same Box, Different Contents

Although men and women may remember things differently, we still store the facts in the same place. How we sort facts and remember events is impacted by our sorting style, regardless of gender.

The following chart (*see next page*) on information sorting styles will add more depth to your thinking about why explanations can differ; consider the impact of gender as you go through it. The chart is based on an analysis of the way people handle information that former Army Ranger Dean Hohl covers in *Rangers Lead the Way*.

LARGE CHUNK		SMALL CHUNK	
big picture		detail oriented	
SEQUENTIAL		RANDOM	
orderly, process oriented		juggler, productive in spite of a messy desk	
POSITIVE		NEGATIVE	
optimist		pessimist	
SAMENESS		DIFFERENCE	
picks up similarities and patterns		picks up contrasts	
I		WE	
define sense of self-worth and own ideas		prefers confirmation from others	
POLARITY RESPONDER		CONFORMITY RESPONDER	
offers alternatives, "devil's advocate"		more likely to agree than offer alternatives	
APPROACH		AVOIDANCE	
actively curious, moves toward the unknown		inhibited, moves away from the unknown	

PAST   PRESENT   FUTURE

EXERCISE 19. SORTING STYLES

OBJECTIVE: See the impact of sorting styles on how a guy answers questions.

This is one to do with friends. A couple of you can ask the guy questions while one of you pays attention to the answers with the sorting styles on page 94 in mind. Choose a topic that invites him to do some storytelling so that you have plenty of chances to figure out if he's sequential or random, positive or negative, and so on.

Get ready to integrate these new skills into a full-bodied strategy for forging a relationship with the man you want.

7.

Observe:
Stage Three Contact

Shift into a more proactive mode now—one in which you use rather high-level interrogator skills not only to find out information, but also to affect outcome. You are about to pass over a threshold that will help you feel confident enough to handle every part of D.E.C.O.D.E.

Approaches

When I use questions, I also try to find what motivates the person to talk to me. In the interrogation business, we call these *approaches*. They are nothing more than lead-ins to encounters that make the prisoner feel comfortable or stressed in way that force him to connect with me. We orchestrate them and weave them into a conversation, often effectively hiding what we really want.

On the following pages are thirteen common approaches with quick definitions; I'll explain them in terms of how

you might use them, as well as how a man might use them with
you:

- **DIRECT** Just ask straight questions with the aim of getting
  straight answers. Don't ask questions that you don't want
  the answer to.
  - ➤ **EXAMPLE** "Where do you see this leading?"
- **INCENTIVE** Offer him something he wants, and use that as a
  trade to get the information you want. Divulge a fact about
  yourself that gets him focused on the kind of information
  you want to know about him.
  - ➤ **EXAMPLE** Try admitting something. "I tried out for cheer-
    leading, but ended up playing clarinet in the band" might
    get him to talk about whether he was popular, geeky, or a
    bad boy in high school.
- **EMOTIONAL** Use the primary categories of emotion—love
  and hate—to engage him either positively or negatively.
  The love and hate are not about you; that's important. They
  are *his* emotions and you are using them to manipulate him
  and get him to talk about something in which his feelings
  dominate, rather than his intellect.
  - **LOVE** You can appeal to someone's love of family or
    friends to make him more or less comfortable.
  - ➤ **EXAMPLE** "You seem to be very close to your sister, but
    the way you talk about your brother—you make him
    sound like a pig."
  - **HATE** You can appeal to someone's hatred of family or
    ex-friends to make him more or less comfortable.
  - ➤ **EXAMPLE** "Your ex-wife should be locked up."

- **FEAR-UP (HARSH)** Yell or do whatever you do to intimidate someone. This approach has no place in your daily life unless you want nothing more than a fight.
  - ➡ **EXAMPLE** You slap him when he insults your mother as a way to try to train him to speak respectfully about your family. (To some men, a harsher gesture would be your bursting into tears and sobbing uncontrollably.)
- **FEAR-UP (MILD)** This could take the form of a veiled threat or making the person feeling as though he's offended you, and then walking out. Question his maturity if he does this to you. Using this on him is not playful. You'd better have a good reason.
  - ➡ **EXAMPLE** "When you insult my mother, you hurt me so much that I may not be able to look at you ever again."
- **FEAR-DOWN** Lower levels of fear or nervousness through comforting words and contact. You're stressed about your first date, so he compliments you and smiles and nods in agreement when you make a point. You see he's nervous, so you make a self-deprecating joke.
  - ➡ **EXAMPLE** "Ignore that remark! I just had a blonde moment!"
- **PRIDE-AND-EGO (UP)** Stroke his ego. Be careful what you want. When you suck up to him, you will send out strong signals.
  - ➡ **EXAMPLE** "You have amazing arms. You must be a bodybuilder."
  - ➡ **EXAMPLE** A man says to a woman who comes into a bar solo, "I can't believe someone as beautiful as you is alone."
- **PRIDE AND EGO (DOWN)** You pretend not to like him or to find some aspect of him to mock in a backhanded way of drawing

him to you. This only works with certain personality types. Remember that there are lots of sensitive men out there— or at least they're sensitive about particular things—and if you hit a raw nerve, you severely damage the rapport.

▶ **EXAMPLE** "You can't possibly think that tattoo is sexy."

■ **FUTILITY** Prey on his doubts, and then cultivate more doubts. You can cash in when it appears you can meet a particular need and eliminate the sense of futility.

> ▶ **EXAMPLE** "That's such a weird habit; I can't imagine too many people putting up with it. Fortunately, I'm used to it because my dad did it." Notice the one-two punch of pride-and-ego (down) and futility.

■ **WE KNOW ALL** Convince someone you know more about him than you do. This is often easy to do as long as you know when to shut up. The trap of the approach is going from sounding intelligent, or at least somewhat knowledgeable about a subject, to babbling.

> ▶ **EXAMPLE** You notice that his eyes keep drifting toward the television, where there's a football game on, and so you later reference a Rose Bowl game in which a spectacular play occurred.

■ **REPETITION** Ask the same question over and over again throughout the conversation. It will drive him nuts, but at some point, he may actually answer it just to shut you up.

■ **ESTABLISH IDENTITY** Get him to tell you something about himself by pretending you already know him. This goes back to one of the oldest pick-up lines in the history of Homo sapiens: "Haven't I seen you somewhere before?"

➡ **EXAMPLE THAT'S NOT SO OBVIOUS** "I know you! I saw you at Hooters last Friday." He looks genuinely surprised and says, "I was at the Lakers game last Friday."

■ **RAPID FIRE** Keep the questions coming, but don't give him a chance to answer. At some point, he will interrupt you and probably give you a more complete answer than you asked for once he gets a few words in edgewise.

➡ **EXAMPLE** "Have you ever hiked in the Rockies? Oh, it's even better in Utah in some ways because the desert has different challenges—have you hiked there? But you know what I love especially about Utah is the free-climbing. Do you like to climb?"

■ **SILENCE** Silence causes the mouth to leak to break the tension. Most people find silence very uncomfortable and, if it occurs during the course of a conversation, they will want to fill the dead air with sound.

➡ **EXAMPLE** "Are you involved?" followed by silence will eventually elicit a response.

EXERCISE 20. APPROACHING APPROACHES

OBJECTIVE: Become aware of how people use approaches in ordinary conversation.

The way you begin to get good at using approaches is to listen to conversations and find out how often people do it naturally. Listen—just listen—to extended conversations between people at meetings, at a bar, or in other situations where someone wants something.

You can, and should, do this with your own family, too. Notice the patterns that you grew up with. Do people in your family use the pride-and-ego (up) to maneuver into Mom's good graces, or use a fear-down approach to get your little brother to go to church with the family?

Questioning Men

Men are good at lying about certain things because of our ability to compartmentalize and because women try so hard to believe us: "No, I did not have an affair" (*Having an affair implies repeated contact. I was with her only once. That's a one-night stand.*) If you combine your improved skills in detecting signs of stress with well-structured questions, you have an excellent chance of getting the straight story. To maximize your chances of hearing the facts, start by asking for the facts. In other words, are you asking the question so you invite a straight answer, or asking the question so you invite the answer you want to hear?

Here is the difference: "You seem to be alone at the party. Do you have a significant other I should know about?"

That's a straight question that will get a straight answer. Compare that to this coy and useless probe: "You are going to introduce me to your wife, aren't you?"

A man hearing the second question knows perfectly well what you want to know, but you have given him permission to compartmentalize. A married man can give you a simple, "No" and continue the flirt. He can also laugh and say, "If I have a wife at this party, it's news to me!" An unmarried man in a committed relationship can ratchet up your expectations with, "I don't have a wife."

Listening for Lies

Your awareness of sorting styles, gender differences in storing information, questions that limit options, and the role of intent in questioning has prepared you for the all-important skill of spotting a liar.

But before you plunge into this new expertise, ask yourself: How valuable is your target? Do you really want to bother with him, or are you engaged in a flirtation without any intention? If it's the latter, then you may not care if he's lying. In fact, I suggest you think of your conversations with him as a game to sharpen your skills at catching liars. Treat every encounter of flirtation, especially the ones that you know will go nowhere, as an opportunity to learn to spot lies. If, on the other hand, this guy has real potential, then you intend to invest emotional energy and time in getting to know this person. You want to know he's telling you the truth.

Flirtatious Lies

Some people just love to flirt. They have no intention of the encounter leading anywhere; they just find flirting fun. A lie told in this context is only completely harmless if both parties have the same mindset. A typical setting for this kind of exchange is a Halloween party, where people have adopted new roles by virtue of their costumes. They come in wearing a lie, so why not have more fun with it?

In contrast, a lot of flirting involves intention on the part of one or both parties. In that case, even a flirtatious lie takes on very negative connotations. Sure, it's common to embellish a little, but when the stories misrepresent you or him in a way that affects your next step, you are headed down a dangerous path. ("Are you free?" "No, but I'm cheap." This bald-faced truth is intended to be flirtatious and cute while at the same time disarming the fact he is cheating.)

To try to figure out whether or not intent is present, start by assuming that he is flirting *without* intent until he takes action to establish intent. He might do that by saying, "This has been fun. Here's my card. I hope you will call or e-mail soon because I'd like to see you again."

In the following scenario, a woman approaches the man. This is not something to avoid necessarily, but keep in mind that if a woman does that, she immediately diminishes any guilt about first contact that a married or committed man might have otherwise had. After that, the woman in the scenario makes the mistake of projecting her intentions on him.

Scenario: Mixed Messages

Mike is attending a computer trade show in Washington, D.C. He's standing at a hotel bar, and an animated woman in a business suit sees his name badge. (She's already removed hers.)

"So they don't let the geeks from the show sit down?" she jokes.

"Now I feel silly," Mike smiles. "All day, I've been telling the guys that I can't wait to get off the floor and put my feet up."

"I'm Jackie, Mike," she says as she extends her hands. "I took my name badge off as I passed the guard at the door."

With an "oops" he whips the badge off with his left hand. She doesn't see a ring—a green light for flirting, as far as she's concerned. Twenty minutes later, the banter has led to lots of laughs and a second round of drinks on the way.

Here's what's going on in his head: *This is so much fun. After living with Megan for six years, I'd forgotten about how good* it feels to flirt with another woman. After all, I'm not really married.

Here's what she's thinking: *This is so much fun. What a great guy! Nothing about him even hints that he's in a relationship. I'd better make sure.*

"So, is your wife in the business, too, Mike?"

At that point, he realizes it's the perfect opportunity to mention Megan's name, but he really wants to keep the flirt going. He says simply, "I'm not married."

Jackie decides to ratchet up the sexual tension a bit. In fact, she does it so much that he starts to get uncomfortable.

Now Mike's head has a different set of thoughts: *I can probably keep this up through the next round, and then I should get out of here. No way I'd cheat on Megan. Room service and a movie sound perfect.*

"Are you going to that conference in Maui next month?" she asks.

Excellent out, he thinks. "Actually, yes. Megan and I thought it would be an opportunity for the company to pay for our vacation."

On hearing a woman's name, Jackie concludes, at first, that he can't be that happy in whatever relationship this is because it took him half an hour to even mention her name. That unfortunate projection of hers leads to another ten minutes of conversation in which he falls into the "we" and "our" speech. She pays the bill and drags her frustration up to her room. *That sonofabitch.*

Technically speaking, Mike told Jackie the truth. In reality, he lied by omission because he wanted to keep the flirt going. That does not make him a bad guy; his objective was to sustain the flirt.

Jackie needs to assume part of the blame for the rocky encounter. Her need for direction in the flirtation signals that she might have a tendency to torpedo her own happiness. In that situation, a woman needs to think of flirting like a ride on a Ferris wheel—going up and down sure is fun. When you get off the ride, you're off the ride. The precise distance you traveled is nowhere.

Unlike Jackie, there are also women who want to be lied to; they make a deceptive exchange into a game. Those women may gladly settle for a one-night stand, or even more, with a married or otherwise committed man. Predatory men pick up on that quickly and oblige with not just one lie but many.

"I'm on to You" Moves

In the interrogation room, I educate my sources that I can read them when they lie. It puts the source on notice that I am on to him and will not tolerate it.

You do not have that artificial construct of control in the dating world that I have during an interrogation, and you'd look like an odd person if you practiced the same behavior in your personal life. You would also be giving away your tools. So, I'm going to give you variations of those tools to call your guy on his crap.

Your body language can insinuate that you're a little suspicious. Most people really do not enjoy lying, and they will build a lie of commission that has its roots in fact. When the story comes to the forefront of conversation, or even gets the spotlight, most will simply try to stop the lie. Some may get so far into the lie they feel they have no option except to continue, but if you catch it early enough, the person will simply extricate himself from the situation or correct his communication.

With a few moves, you can help stop it before it goes so far that neither of you can recover. As a natural response to these moves, your guy will be impelled to explain further because he detects on either a conscious or subconscious level that you question what he said. Actions that will help you get that result include:

- Raise both eyebrows a little when something sounds embellished or incorrect. Hold your brows in the raised position for a few seconds.
- Raise one eyebrow as *Star Trek*'s Mr. Spock does when he says to James T. Kirk, "Interesting, Captain."
- Close one eyelid tightly as you wrinkle your nose.
- Just wrinkle your nose.
- Tighten your brow.
- Roll your eyes.
- Run your tongue over the outside of your teeth (lips closed).

Try to create your own list. You may have to resort to something more full-bodied if Fred Flintstone does not get it. One move: Draw away from him just enough so that he notices the distance.

Fabrication Versus Distortion

A lie requires intent, and distortion is often a side effect of the intensity of an event. When I interrogate a soldier who tells me he walked through the mountains for sixty miles with a hundred pounds on his back, I ask a few simple questions beginning with, "Man, that must have been hard. Who else was with you?" If he is fabricating, and he knows I have the ability to check with his comrades, he will come clean here. Otherwise, I ask, "What were you carrying that weighed so much? Your underwear must be made of chain maille!" Maybe he'll say that he had a radio and full ammo load, so I'll challenge him on distance: "Where did you end up? What was your starting point?" In short, his story holds up in terms of the weight carried, but I surmise that the heavy load distorted his perception of distance. It's not a matter of his lying; it's a matter of his not knowing the truth.

Emotions and general state of mind distort the facts. If I am exhausted, my story will take on an air of difficulty. If I am exhausted and victorious, it will take shape differently. Think of your daily life and how much impact one negative event can have on the rest of the day. An unrelated chain of events can mysteriously seem to conspire against you. The fact is that one incident distorted your reactions to the others, and you may have even caused the subsequent events.

EXERCISE 21. EXPLORE DISTORTION

OBJECTIVE: Tune in to how people distort the facts.

Think of an event you have in common with friends, such as your high school prom or a trip you took together. Write down the facts as you remember them. Ask your friends to do the same. Compare notes. When the exercise is over, let it go. Do not try to figure out whose story is the "most correct."

To gain a better understanding of distortion, think about your last "great" relationship—and how it ended. The way a relationship ends will distort how you see the relationship.

Tactics for Breaking a Liar

- Find the critical points, or critical junctures, in the story. Pull them out and ask about them. Your life is like a photo album with shots that overlap. Most lies are more like stand-alone snapshots. The details that link the pieces break stories.

EXERCISE 22. DISTORTION VERSUS LIES

OBJECTIVE: See how much impact stress and emotion have on remembering the facts.

Sit with someone you know well, otherwise you may offend the person with this one. Ask about the most physically or psychologically stressful thing she has ever experienced. If it was a truly stressful event, the memory of it will very likely contain some distortion of the facts. When you get to critical points of the story, like distance or duration, ask questions that will clarify your understanding of how she is sure. Ask questions such as these:

- You ran thirty miles? When? Where? Why?
- What was the terrain like?
- How did you know it was thirty miles?
- Where did you keep your water?

At the end, point out to your friend what you thought *might* be a deviation from the facts. And make it clear that it's normal to misremember events in the face of stress so that she doesn't feel like a liar.

- The technique of questioning about critical points works best with lies of embellishment and transference. Examples in a story about kayaking would include the type of kayak, other boat traffic, distance traveled, and temperature.

■ Use the forward and backward pass, project management phrases for tracking a timeline forward and backward. A critical path expresses what has to happen in which order; a forward pass of the critical path will help you look at things in the order in which they are supposed to occur. A backward pass moves along the same critical path in reverse. And, as in project management, you will find errors going backward that you could never find going forward.

  - This works well with lies of commission and omission, which frequently involve some premeditation. Let's say the story centers on a trip to Paris. You strongly suspect that he did not make the trip alone, yet he keeps talking about "I," not "we." His story skips from an afternoon visit to the Louvre to a boat ride on the Seine that night. You might detect a lie if you hear an improbable or weak answer to "Where did you go right after the Louvre?" If he says, "I went shopping," you might want to hold on to your suspicions as you quiz him about which stores he stopped in and what he bought.

  - You can combine the forward and backward pass—questions about when things occurred, what occurred, in what sequence events occurred—with your knowledge of sorting styles.

■ Ask questions that involve different senses. Most people have a dominant sense they rely on to soak in information.

I'm auditory, so in school I responded well to lectures; I really enjoy music. Many more people are visual; their access sense is sight. If you ask them questions that force them to draw on another sense, if they really had the experience, they might be able to do it. Then again, if the person clearly talks mostly about the sounds and the feel (kinesthetic sense) of an experience, and suddenly adds massive visual detail, you might wonder how much that is coming from the construct side of his brain.

- Use his memory keys against him. Is he time-driven, sequence-driven, or event driven?

Breaking a Liar

Most liars do not need drama to know they have been caught. They leak signs of guilt, which include the use of adaptors, the body language that helps a person try to cope with stress.

The first thing to remember when trying to detect a lie is to listen for content. Keep track of the elements of the story that involve things you know about. If a man says he ran the New York City Marathon on November 5, draw on your knowledge of New York, running, and November weather on the East Coast.

Second, ask questions about the details. This will drive most men crazy because they think that you are derailing the conversation, but it can help you detect a lie:

HIM: I killed nine men with an eyelash.
YOU: What color was the eyelash?

The following story involves all four kinds of lies: omission, commission, transference, and embellishment. After you read it—and before I give you a sample scenario on breaking the liar—think about what you would do to detect each kind of lie. There are myriad possibilities using the two techniques just mentioned.

The setting is a Christmastime cocktail reception at an art gallery. You met Bill at the hors d'oeuvres tray about ten minutes ago, and he shows all the signs of being attracted to you. From your perspective, he's good-looking, manly, and well dressed, with a wonderful smile and hearty laugh. He tells you this story.

"I went snowshoeing at midnight with a group of twelve people. I should say, I *brought* snowshoes, even though I don't like them much. I figured I'd wear my skis unless the snow was really deep. There was a full moon—unbelievable how it lit up the path. The path wound through huge trees, uphill for eight miles.

"Even some of the guys who'd been on snowshoes a lot had a hard time because the path was so steep. I had no problem at all on my skis, though. The trail came out on a frozen lake. The wind blasted us as soon as we broke out of the trees, but we got to see the most amazing thing. The moon was shining on the lake. It was so bright; it was like a spotlight.

"There was one couple with us—this was so funny—she said really loud so her boyfriend could hear her over the wind: 'Wouldn't this be a great place to get married?' Just about everybody heard it, and we all went, 'Awwww, get a room.'

"Then we turned around and headed down the path. I swear I had more fun than anybody on those skis. For one thing, I made it down about half an hour before the rest of them."

Keep in mind that lies of embellishment are the most common. If you suspected that any part of the story wasn't exactly true, your first thought might be that he simply exaggerated a few facts. You would immediately go to parts of the story that related to difficulty, such as the distance from the trailhead to the lake, how hard the wind blew, and how challenging the path was—especially to someone on skis.

Here is how you might use the four elements of detecting a lie (critical points, forward and backward pass, access sense, and sorting styles to break the liar) to break the liar.

Critical Point #1: Length of Trail

The first point to focus on is the length of the trail.

YOU: Which trail did you take? (You know some trails in the area, so this is a strong start, but it can be a critical point whether or not you have any familiarity with the trails. *He does not know what you know*, so you can still see the stress signals, such as adaptors, if he has not thought of the answer.)

BILL: The one that starts at Glacier Gorge trailhead and ends up at the Loch.

YOU: Gosh, it's further to the lake than I thought.

BILL: Have you ever been on it in winter?

YOU: No.

BILL: You have to divert part way up, so it's a lot longer.

You think that the trail is more like four miles up and four miles back. He would have had to take quite a detour to double the length. You suspect a bit of embellishment, but you aren't sure. That exaggeration can be, in part, a physiological response to the physical demands distorting his perception. More likely, it's a bit of bravado. "I skied uphill for eight miles," is the gist of this story, after all.

Critical Point #2: The Full Moon
Next, you could focus on the full moon.

YOU: When did you do the trek?
BILL: Three weeks ago. The day before Thanksgiving.

You have the Weather Channel desktop software on your computer, so you have a keen sense of when full moons occur. The moon wasn't quite there yet the day before Thanksgiving. Another embellishment.

Critical Point #3: The Composition of His Group
Next, you could focus on the composition of the group, using the information he gave you.

YOU: The image of the lake must have been stunning! Sounds like it was wasted on almost everybody except the one couple. What was this—a bunch of guys going for a midnight hike with flasks of brandy?
BILL: No, there were other couples there, too. In fact, it was mostly couples.

He strongly suggested that there was only one couple. Now you suspect a lie of omission. Was he part of a couple that night?

Critical Point #4: The Skis
Now, move on to the point of the skis.

YOU: And you on skis? I can see using the skis on the downhill part, but uphill?

BILL: Yeah, I've lived on skis in the winter since I was four years old.

YOU: How did you go uphill eight miles in skis?

BILL: Actually, it's easy.

You suspect it's a lie of either commission or transference.

Critical Point #5: Going Uphill on Skis
If he had really skied uphill, you think, he would have answered the question "how." So, you ask it again.

YOU: Maybe for you, but I don't have a clue how you do that.

BILL: It's—hang on just a second. I have to give my buddy, Eric, over there his drink tickets. I will be back in ten seconds!

You know that Eric owns the sporting goods store on Main Street. Now you are convinced that Bill's lie is one of either commission or transference, probably the latter. Eric would definitely know how to go uphill in skis.

Critical Point #6: Time-Distance Relationship

Once Bill returns to the conversation, you can get him to divulge more information in order to further incriminate himself. In this case, he could present a time-distance relationship that doesn't add up.

> **BILL:** As I was saying, you use climbing skins that you take off on the way down.
>
> **YOU:** How long did it take the normal people to get back down the trail?
>
> **BILL:** Ninety minutes.

You've been on snowshoes going downhill. Unless the people on snowshoes spent some of the time sliding down icy patches on their butts, there is no way they could manage the downhill portion of an eight-mile hike in ninety minutes. Conversely, on skis, the downhill trip should be swift, getting him to the trailhead with far more than a thirty-minute margin. You've caught him in a lie of commission.

Listen for signs of the person emphasizing a point for no apparent reason—"I swear to God that was the most spectacular frozen lake I've ever seen." That can also indicate that the story has been spiced with a little exaggeration.

Some people are more tied to sequence or events than time, for example. So do not presume that an incorrect, or even nonsensical, response to a time question makes the person a liar. Watch for adaptors, including vocal adaptors like a cadence shift, which signal that some stress is leaking. That's the relevant indicator, much more so than the lousy answer. A lot of people can't remember details, but they won't be stressed over it if the story is true.

Women accept distortions from men all the time, or at least they don't correct them. A guy gives you lines about his life and experiences, and you just sit there and say, "Wow." All you've done is invited him to pile up more crap like a dung beetle. Please stop it.

At the same time, do not assume that a questionable answer is a lie. After all, if a man is under stress, then you might be, too. That can affect your listening as much as it affects his telling.

Interrogation can be a genuinely high-stress encounter because both the environment and the information in play may involve stress. In contrast, unless your date a pilot practicing stall maneuvers, the main source of stress in your encounter is the information in play. He may be stressed in telling you a story because he's nervous around you, or the story itself may involve a psychologically or physically demanding event. Because he was under stress when he had the experience, it is likely to distort the facts in his mind. Lying requires intent, so even though he isn't exactly telling the truth, he isn't lying either.

EXERCISE 23. TRUE LIES

OBJECTIVE: Use the four tools to practice breaking a liar.

Have someone you know lie to you. Urge the person to make the story as believable as possible. This will probably mean that the person will use embellishment and transference to concoct something because they are relatively easy ways to lie well. Use the tools of critical points, forward and backward pass, access sense, and sorting styles to break the liar. Simply make mental notes about what you think are the false parts of the story, and ask your friend to tell you afterward which were lies.

Whether a man always finds flirting itself a high-stress situation or you encounter a man in a genuinely high-stress event (a
funeral, the emergency room), you need to keep your head if you
find him attractive.

Spot the Rituals

Rituals can be automatic responses you picked up from your family, religion, or culture, or they could be things you do deliberately. An example might be the way a man touches your face to
suggest the need for a kiss, or maybe he subconsciously puts his
hand at the small of your back before he moves in to kiss you.
On the same subconscious level, you pick up the signal each and
every time.

Humans operate on autopilot through much of our lives.
There are many things we do consciously, but others just happen.
Regardless of whether or not we started out doing them intentionally, at some point, we slipped into autopilot. Take brushing
your teeth, for instance. While not exactly a ritual in that way
we're defining it here, do you realize how you do it? If you know
exactly how you brush your teeth and the steps are thought out
and intentional, it has been way too long. You need a date now.

Brushing your teeth indicates how things can become an auto
response. Now overlay that onto the rest of your life. What other
things have become automatic? How you eat? The preparations
related to sleeping? The invitation and response to a kiss? The
cues for sexual intimacy?

In teaching interrogators, I always say there are three primal drives in humans that, if interfered with, have dire consequences: food, sleep, and sex. When one is withheld, a person will over-compensate, either by overindulging in the withheld thing at the first opportunity or by replacing it with one of the other two. On a subconscious level, they have an almost religious significance to most humans, and rituals evolve around how we deal with each.

Rituals are pathways to putting ourselves into a new place to prepare for these primal drives. They are routines of lesser activities that separate special things into a space of their own.

Look at your food ritual. When you are getting ready for dinner, what is your process? There may be a cleansing activity, that is, you wash your hands regardless of whether you are at home, at a friend's house, or at a restaurant. Do you always set the table the same way? You might think, "Well, of course I do. There's only one way to do it!" But is there even an order in which you place the settings? Your mother taught you well; she sowed a ritual into your life. These are the kind of habits that have such significance that, if interrupted, there are emotional consequences for you.

A ritual is not simply a habit like cracking your knuckles; it's something with meaning. Setting a table differently from the way your mother taught you might cause you feel disconnected from your upbringing and from propriety. Such rituals are a cluster of habits that are not simply repeated at random times but are repeated instead around an event of significance. In this case, it's eating. This cluster of habits actually impacts the outcome of the event and the quality of the experience. Our feeding rituals likely started at the breast, and our mothers evolved them from there.

And unlike table setting, many of them are so ingrained that we are not even aware of them.

When a ritual involves another person, it is typically a learned behavior created by positive or negative reinforcement from another person. These rituals continue to evolve throughout someone's life if the person stays in the same relationship. The rituals tend to be specialized, attuned to that microculture of two people. Even though some cues of the ritual are universal among humans—batting eyelashes, tilting the head in a submissive posture—these cues can become distorted through positive and negative reinforcement.

For example, think of the couple that has had many ugly fights leading to hot sex as part of the making-up process. They may subconsciously get to the point in their rituals where they fight to bring on great sex. Is this normal? For them it is. But when one of them leaves that relationship and tries to replicate the passion, that's probably the start of a disaster. You need to experience the benefits of this ritual first to see the reasons for continuing it.

Sex rituals, or indicators that you have said "yes" to the dance, are complex. What is acceptable, what is the direction, what are the limits implied—all of these elements, and many more, define the rituals.

Early in the dating process, your rituals may revolve around friends and activities outside the home. These cause you to draw together, but as the relationship develops, the rituals move to encompass intimate details. What you habitually do together draws you closer. You develop cues for when it is time to continue to party, time to leave, time to be quiet.

On the negative side, one person may have residual rituals that suggest an argument is about to start. It's like an actor coming onto a set and recognizing everything is ready for the fight scene. But the actors are different. The story is different. The audience is different. Nevertheless, if you present that same set of indicators, then the fight is on. Remember the last big fight you had with a boyfriend or husband? How much of the fight was real, and how much was a compounding of the issue with the ritual of argument?

Ritualistic Adaptation

Rituals take our minds from one state of being to another. They take us out of our normal activity and prepare us for something very different.

We can raise adaptors, or stress-relieving gestures, to a point that they look very much like rituals. Watch how animals use ritual to relieve stress. Dogs scratch obsessively or pace back and forth. A bird might pluck his feathers. Watch a captive creature and you will see the living meaning of "behaving like a caged animal."

Human stress rituals have the same soothing effect. You'll see that individuals get addicted to certain actions; the actions become "their way" of dealing with a strange environment or an increased level of anxiety.

If you look at anything you and friends do habitually when you're together, from table manners to way you greet someone when she comes to your door, you will spot a ritual that's designed to make you and others more comfortable.

Family practices and personal experiences also lie at the heart of many of adult stress rituals. If you were a thumb-sucking, hair-stroking, or foot-tapping kid, you may still be doing that. And if you are not doing that specific action to calm yourself, you're probably doing a variation of it. The thumb-sucker might bring her thumb to her chin during a business meeting. On a date, the hair-stroker might put her hand on her neck. The foot-tapper might wiggle his toes in his shoes.

What if a guy is a foot-tapper and I put him in the cloistered environment of an interrogation room—a place designed to ratchet up his stress level? How different is that from the increased stress level of a first meeting with someone he thinks is hot, or a first date with the girl of his dreams? On that first date, his ritual will become even more pronounced than it usually is. In a staged encounter like a date, nothing is familiar at first except his weird little ritual. You will also see it when, for example, a neat person has to experience some social event in a cluttered environment. So if your apartment is a mess, watch for the signs. In an episode of *Friends*, Ross goes to the apartment of a gorgeous woman who has dirty clothes and last week's dinners between her couch cushions. A meticulous metrosexual and scientist, he freaks out and his nonstop nervous giggles don't hide his stress.

If I'm interrogating a Ross who has suddenly been subjected to clutter, he may start out by giggling, but that habit might join a party of rituals such as foot-tapping, brushing his pants, buttoning and re-buttoning his shirt cuffs, and moving his fingers across the table to remove dust. He would try to order what he could, to gain control over the structure of his environment to whatever extent possible.

EXERCISE 24. RITUAL OR WEIRD HABIT

OBJECTIVE: Get a grasp on your behavior patterns to determine what serves you and what's extra.

You may crack your knuckles regularly because it feels good, or you may do it because you are facing something stressful. One is a habit, and the other is a ritualistic adaptor. In this exercise, look at your life from the point of view of ritual versus habit. Make a list, with rituals in your life in one column and habits in the other.

Food: What do you consistently do before every meal? After? Does it bother you if it is interfered with? Does it affect your perception of the quality of the meal?

Sleep: Outline your regular process for getting to bed and then to sleep. What happens if a deviation occurs? Does it damage the quality of your sleep? What fairly ordinary disruptions (as opposed to a bomb going off next door) prevent you from getting sleep?

Sex: What is the sequence of steps someone takes that lures you toward sex? When you initiate the process, what do you do?

Argument: What are the keys to you that a conversation is deteriorating into a fight? What is your trip wire—the point of no return for you?

Although it can vary with family practice and culture, Americans generally reserve eighteen inches or less of space for intimate contact. If someone moves in past this space, either you have invited him through your body language or you will feel that his action is threatening.

Americans traveling abroad often find the close contact of people in the streets as odd, and they might sometimes even see it as part of a sexual ritual. But the elements of American sexual ritual actually do not involve intimate contact; this is obvious to the trained eye. Simply holding hands does not indicate intimacy, and neither does an arm around someone. When you mirror the other person, making your body move like the other person's, that is a more substantial signal. Mirroring subconsciously puts the other person at ease. The seduction dance involves mirroring done at a noticeably slow pace, with exaggerated movements done in an almost lethargic manner. If you videoed the interaction and played it back at a fast speed, you would find the movements as bizarre as a movie from the 1920s. Hands curl to make each person appear less threatening, heads tilt, eyes are open. Blood flow to mucosa increases in response to the surge in hormones, so eyes dilate to take in more information, lips become fuller, and faces flush. As this progresses, the sexually aroused couple begins to match cadence, and the ritual is complete.

In an intimate relationship, you regularly conduct rituals that lead to lowering defenses and opening up to your date. If these rituals suddenly feel stilted or out of sequence, stay alert for other signs that the relationship is off track. A break in rituals is not a sure sign of infidelity, but it does indicate that something is commanding a good deal of your man's attention.

EXERCISE 25. YOUR MATING RITUALS

OBJECTIVE: Identify the rituals you and your guy have regarding food, sex, and sleep.

Does he pull your chair out when you sit down every time you have dinner together? Always sleep on the same side of the bed? Always undress starting with the shirt and working his way down? Make a list of the rituals that occur when you are together—anything that seems like a stabilizing behavior pattern within the context of the relationship.

Now, let's assume that you're sleeping with the guy. If you aren't, you still have every reason to read on because you will probably sleep with him, or somebody, one of these days.

Your sleep rituals involve any number of actions: what kind of pillow you use, how you angle it, how many blankets you pile on, and which side of the bed you sleep on. The rituals begin even before you get into bed. A break with your nighttime routine can indicate whether or not you're at ease.

If you prey upon someone's rituals to tantalize, and then withhold food, sex, or sleep, for example, the result is displaced expectations. In the interrogation room, it makes prisoners more vulnerable. In the bedroom, it can make people angry, so be careful.

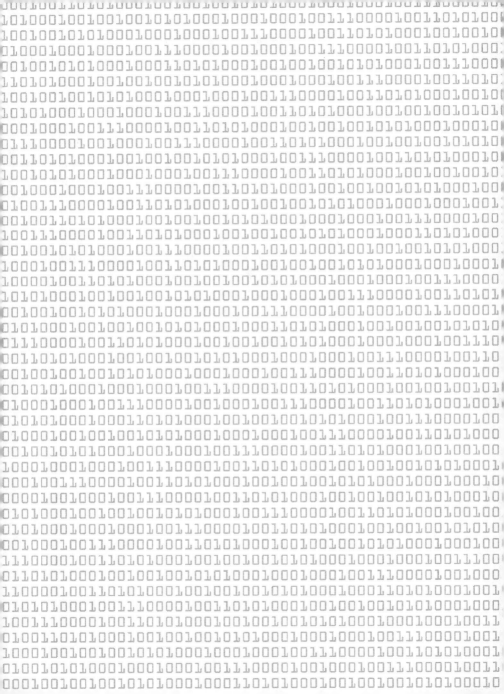

8.

Observe:
The Mating Dance

The illustrations in this chapter are based on photos I took of three different sets of male-female interactions in a bar. With you in mind, I set out to log the flow of a ritual mating dance so I could show you the sequence of events that occurs in bars, at parties, and at other social gatherings every day.

I did my research for this chapter in a very popular, big-city bar with a clientele ranging in age from barely legal to people (mostly men) in their sixties. I would not call it a meat market, but I would say that the atmosphere invited connections. In other words, after five o'clock, you probably wouldn't bring the family there for burgers.

The First Dance

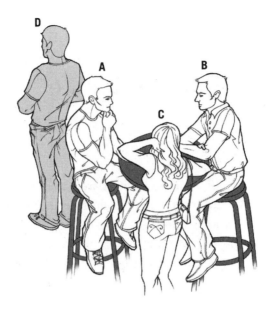

A handsome young man (**A**) and his older friend (**B**) are sitting and talking. The young guy has a good physique, great features—the all-American type—and is probably the best-looking man in the bar. A young woman (**C**), who doesn't appear to know either of them, starts to talk to them. They invite her to sit down. Physically, the young man and woman appear to be a good match, and from the moment she joins the table she sends signal after signal that she finds him attractive: hair flipping, neck stroking, angling her body toward him. You don't need this book to know that she's putting it all out for him. He turns his whole body toward her, facing her openly with his chest and his legs casually open. Neither one puts a barrier between them.

Another man (**D**), eyeing the attractive young woman, moves closer to the table, but keeps his back to it—and to her. **D** flares his shoulders and stands square, with feet firmly planted beneath his shoulders, so he exposes the young woman to a hyper-masculine pose.

Men recognize this kind of plumage ruffling (and now, so do you). An uninterested man at another table looks at **D** suspiciously, as if he's thinking, "Yeah, I know what you're trying to do, buddy."

The ritual dance between the young man and woman gears up as follows: His openness to her indicates that he wants a connection with her. As she continues her head tilts and playing with her hair, however, the young man shows signs that he has no idea that she feels attracted to him, too. He resorts to a kind of goofball, locker-room approach to flirting: tossing bits of ice and straws at her. She responds by playfully punching him in the arm. He's doing a ritualistic adaptation, that is, things that have worked for him in the past to get the girl. She's engaging in adaptive behavior by mirroring his style of playfulness. In a manner typical of young men, he demonstrates that he does not get her message; he continues selling. He's oblivious, even though she's done everything except say out loud, "You've sold me. You've closed the deal. Now let's move on."

When I'm teaching a mixed group of young interrogators about body language, I ask the women in the class, "What's the number-one mistake that men make in a pick-up situation?" "They don't know when they've won," they respond, "so they don't know when to shut up." I explain that men almost always think more is better. We use more nails, more screws, and more cologne than we need. Commonly, we also overdo whatever we think will impress a woman we feel sexually attracted to.

While the protracted flirtation is going on, the older friend has consistently had his arm on the table between him and the young woman. It's a definite barrier and very likely his subconscious way of saying to the young man, "She's yours. I have no intention of coming on to her." The woman is in a cooperation zone.

Both men and women set up competition and cooperation zones. When men decide to cooperate with each other so that one of them "snares" you, you're in trouble if you don't spot it early on. They have already agreed that one of them will get you and want to get that done—maybe just to prove they can. One might pretend to go after your girlfriend, for example, as part of his buddy's scheme to hook up with you. In contrast to the cooperation scheme, men who are competing for you will not help each other. They want you more than they want to play a game in which they're teammates. In fact, the new game may become "I want her" and/or "You can't have her." This is where the term *cockblock* comes from.

Another young man (**1**) sees the young woman at the table. Recognizing her, he approaches and begins a conversation. She talks to him, but keeps her focus on **A.**

At the same time, **D**—still with his back to the table and holding his macho-man posture—remains on target. A slight head turn indicates he might be listening; it's as though he has overheard something of interest.

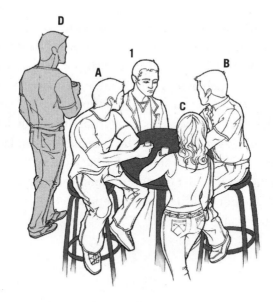

While **1**, clearly a friend of the young woman's, settles in at the table, **A** goes to the bar to get drinks for himself and for her.

Stay tuned, while I switch to another storyline developing near the area of the bar where **A** has gone.

The Second Dance

A young man (**2**) who entered the bar with two other guys (**1** and **3**) quickly engages two women in conversation. One is a very attractive platinum blonde (**5**), well-dressed and sure of herself. The other is relatively plain (**6**) and wearing a shirt too tight for her physique. She appears to be almost protective of her pretty friend; that's like protecting a shark from swimmers.

The man (**2**) is obviously not the alpha in the group, but he seizes an opportunity to move on the pretty blonde when his alpha friend (**1**) notices a friend at a nearby table (the table where the First Dance is occurring). The blonde temporarily entertains the approach of **2** and even laughs at his joke loudly. She uses her friend as a barrier, and she turns away from him as she laughs. He doesn't notice, however, because he is leaning back, laughing at his own joke. Notice how **3** spreads his back (lat spread to appear more masculine); he can't carry it off, and the effect makes him look almost wooden. Of the three, he appears to be the least confident around women.

Shift your attention to the previous illustration as you go through this description. At one point, the young man (**2**) moves in closer to the tables. The blonde woman moves around the table allowing her friend (**6**) to change positions as well, thereby remaining the barrier. The blonde is no fool and truly understands setting limits on personal space. By now, the more confidant man (**1**) has returned and started a conversation with the blonde. Guy **2** realizes—through a combination of her clues and the presence of the alpha—that he should concentrate on the friend (**6**). You know where that is going to lead. She still appears mildly interested in his conversation; he probably has not let her know yet that she is now his choice, because he could not get the first one. Poor man (**3**) is still just hanging out with nobody, but look at how his body language mirrors the recently returned alpha. ("If my buddy can get the girl with his hands in his pockets, then maybe I should . . .) But look who else is in this illustration (**D**), and the shift in dynamics that has occurred while **A** is at the bar.

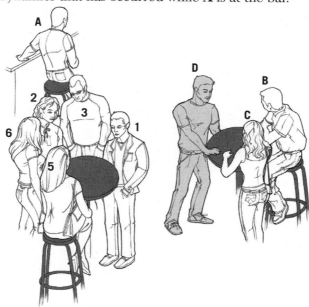

The First Dance Redux

When **A** went to the bar, he had a lot of reasons to be confident that the young women would still be there when he got back. First of all, he was buying her a drink. Secondly, he had his friend at the table to keep an eye on her. Third, he was starting to get that maybe she liked him.

How could he know that the opportunistic bottom feeder (**D**) would turn around and start talking directly to her? Here is a man who is not too stupid when it comes to moving in. He picked up that **A** didn't know enough to close the deal when he had a chance, that he did nothing to assert himself when the woman's friend came over, and that he didn't notice that he might have a rival for her attention, namely, himself. He makes his play.

She's polite but throws up barriers immediately. Shortly after **A** returns, and before they finish their drinks, the two of them leave together. I didn't overhear the conversation, but she could have easily done a graceful equivalent of "You've got me," by saying something like, "That creep tried to hit on me. Could we please go somewhere else and talk?"

The Second Dance Redux

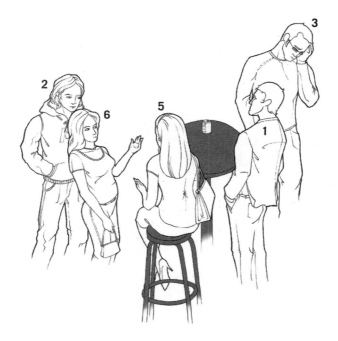

Alpha man (**1**) is savvy about women like our blonde star. He realizes the others are wasting money on her and turns his attention to the band. For her part, the blonde recognizes his type as well and firmly places a barrier in the form of a large bag over her shoulder in his direction. As a further barrier, she leans away to put more distance between them. By now man **2** has made his move and lost the interest of woman **6**: She is barriering by holding her glass higher than normal and looking away.

Poor man **3** walks away rubbing his temples in either disgust or confusion. He never was in the game.

The blonde shark unquestionably controls the conversation. When she decides the party is over, the two women exit after a very inexpensive, if not fulfilling, evening. They got drinks out of the deal, as well as flowers the men bought them from a vendor strolling through the bar. They leave alone.

The Third Dance

This one has a single important point: Even a drunk, inexperienced young woman can, and should, push back when her personal space is invaded.

At first, I had an urge to intervene with this one because **X** was clearly trying to take advantage of **Y,** who was probably too young to even be in the bar. She accepted a couple of drinks from him and seemed to lose some control. He wanted payback for his investment and moved in closer and closer until his invasion went well into dangerous territory: the eighteen-inch comfort zone. Fortunately, it did not take her long to say a quick goodbye and head for the door.

Your Next Dance

I invite you to take a pen with you and start drawing your own illustrations on cocktail napkins. (It's a little more discreet than using your cell phone to photograph people picking each other up.)

Watch for barriers, illustrators, plumage ruffling, and other elements of the ritual mating dance. Make a game out of it with your friends: Take bets on who gets lucky and who gets dumped. It will raise your personal awareness of where you stand and what intentions you're conveying when you encounter a man you want to take home.

Two words probably came to mind as I described the interaction of the people in that bar: games and sex. The games, of course, are what you do to get the sex, or to use the vaguer phrase of today, to hook up.

The games men play can tell you a lot about whether or not they bring value to the situation. The type of sex that's preoccupying their thoughts at the moment will affect how they treat you. Their intentions will leak and help you make choices about them.

Real Value or Late-Night Infomercial

Criss Angel, of the television show *Mindfreak,* stuns audiences with his levitation. He appears to float onto a chair or a low wall. Angel explains his trick, which is simple, by emphasizing the importance of misdirection of attention. He masks critical points just as a good liar would. One shoe is attached to his pants leg; that pants leg has an opening that allows Angel to slip his leg out and step onto the object in front of him. With the audience behind him, it appears that his lower body floats onto the chair. Angel extends his arms as though he's about to fly and talks to the audience while he quickly makes his move: He misdirects their attention to his upper body while his lower body does the trick.

The dating scene is full of guys who think they can dazzle like Criss Angel. They have their slick moves; they get your attention with one hand while doing something with the other. If I yell and stomp my feet during an interrogation, I might be hiding something that I do not want the source to discover. When I shout, it's primarily to hide a psychological gambit that I've set up. I want the source to work on fending me off rather than focus on my argument. It keeps him off-balance so that he goes toward an emotional state and away from a cognitive one; his ability to perceive what I'm really doing to him is diminished. The result is that I have more control over him.

Consider the story of author Terry McMillan, author of *How Stella Got Her Groove Back,* for a moment. Jonathan Plummer, the source of McMillan's groove, may have used misdirection to cover up his hidden agenda of gaining access to her money, as well as his homosexuality. Exactly what does a gay man look like?

Well, he looks like a man who likes men. There is no great indicator other than the physical tells that he is attracted. The dilemma of spotting his preference was a difficult one, and the sleight of hand in this case was the affection he showed Terry.

Put yourself in her position. Knowing what you know now about voluntary and involuntary body responses, you would watch for involuntary responses if you had the slightest suspicion about the man's gender preference. Even a skilled cover-up artist could not hide blood flow to the lips and softening of the eyes that occur when sexual attraction kicks in. Add to that the too-long eye contact, slowed cadence, and mirroring that complete the picture. You see him respond to a man like that, and you have him pegged. You know the secrets so you can detect that his heterosexuality is just a trick, like Angel's levitation.

It is often true that information and/or skill equals value. But does entertainment equal value? Fun facts. Magic tricks. ESP games. Both men and women do it: This is a simple differentiating-myself-from-the-masses exercise. It's an answer to the question, "Why am I more valuable than the rest of these chimps?" In evolutionary terms, the male monkey who appeared to be more valuable—stronger, smellier, bigger—got the girl. The female who looked like she could produce the stronger, smellier, bigger offspring got the guy. Those days are gone for us and replaced by a much more sophisticated dance. Value can be demonstrated in countless ways. I have a friend who, in his youth, learned to bite a chunk out of beer mugs without injuring himself—something he has little use for as he approaches fifty.

The way men convey their "value information"—the way they present the tricks—can tell you a lot about the real person, however. To get past the sleight of hand, you need to use your knowledge of personality types and styles of sorting information, as well as apply your newfound skills in reading body language. By doing that, you can learn to use their gimmicks as a way of discovering the real person. You may end up concluding that the guy is an incorrigible playboy or emotional midget, and look at him in your rearview mirror as you mutter, "I know what you tried to do and it was lame." Or you may begin to detect his true value. You may find a crack in the persona, peek in, and conclude that you are dealing with a decent, vulnerable human being.

So much of the effectiveness of a demonstration of real or perceived value relates to context. A friend of mine, who did public relations for a company that staged computer conferences, had drinks after the conference with a group of attendees. Unlike my friend, they lived and breathed computers. When a very high-profile man in this community—a software guru—pontificated in her direction, she ignored him. He ruffled his plumage a little more by allowing the adoring members of his entourage to compliment him, and then moved on her again. He was nobody to her. His gimmick fell flat. Had she had a real connection to, and respect for, the people who fawned all over him, she might have been influenced to accept the come-on, however.

The following exercise should put you on the path to understanding if you are being taken in by the guy you're dating. Don't do it with him, though; this is about how easily you're duped. Do you easily get sucked in by the reactions of other people to a guy with great gimmicks? In other words, is he a stand-up comic who gets your laugh because you want to laugh with the rest of the crowd?

EXERCISE 26. FLOATING DEBRIS OR TIP OF THE ICEBERG

OBJECTIVE: Find out how gullible you are.

Observe someone who has prepared his opener. I do not mean a simple pick-up line. I mean an opening gimmick like an Atlanta Braves team outfit—hat, jacket, T-shirt—or a card trick. Ask him how he learned the card trick, whether or not it's his only card trick, and what drew him to this particular card trick over any others. How long did it take him to learn it? You want to use questioning like this to determine whether his gimmick is just a bunch of facts or it's really part of him. Dustin Hoffman, as Raymond Babbitt, the savant with autism in *Rain Man*, can reel off statistics on airline accidents, but that didn't make him a pilot or an FAA executive. There are tons of armchair quarterbacks out there who can tell you how football is played but never play the game.

Draw on your questioning skills and use the following to determine the "truth" of his gimmick:

- Critical points
- Forward and backward pass
- Access senses
- Memory key
- Sorting styles

I always say any idiot can ask enough questions to make a wise man look like a fool. You are going to stop just short of that.

If he is like most people who use the gimmick as an ice breaker, he will probably see your questions as an expression of interest in him, an opportunity to move on to more useful conversation. In some way, he will admit it is just plumage ruffling, which is fine. If he is a master manipulator, however, he will likely make some reference to his Jedi-like mind skills, something akin to "I'm the only one I know who can do this." Be wary of that guy. Another possibility: If he is genuinely into sleight of hand, or whatever his gimmick is, his passion will show, and you will soon hear more about card tricks than any normal woman would want to know. He's just excited that you're interested and wants to share what he knows. Whatever the result, you will have a better insight into the man. This line of questioning will work for any subject. You do not need to know anything about ant farming to find out how much it means to him.

The Men Behind the Magic

When considering men's value, they essentially fall in three categories.

First, a man can have real value, to you or someone else, and easily demonstrate it. For example, let's say he is polite. You notice in the way he treats friends, strangers, and you that this is a consistent, comfortable part of his behavior. Even more obvious examples are handsome, famous, and well built. All a gorgeous movie star has to do to demonstrate value is stand in a room. He has value on two fronts: looks and wealth. Is he hiding something more special, or is that enough?

Second, a man can have real value, but he cannot easily demonstrate it—either because he does not know how, or because the "wow" thing he has to offer isn't easily demonstrated. Let's say he loves children, and as a pediatric oncologist, his passion is saving them from the ravages of cancer. If he isn't comfortable talking about his work, how is he going to demonstrate his value in a bar? Another example would be financial genius. How does the chief financial officer of a *Fortune* 500 company demonstrate value at a party where nobody knows him?

Last, a man can have no value, but he can still know well how to *demonstrate* value. Con men and psychopaths fit into this category.

As I said in the introduction to these sections, the games men play can tell you whether or not they bring real value. At the same time, it's the type of sex that's preoccupying their thoughts that will affect how they treat you.

What Kind of Sex?

I believe the second most powerful drive in humans is to conquer, which stands right behind the need to reproduce. Even as we age, the drive persists in some form. Ask any healthy adolescent boy, and he'll assure you that reproduction is definitely not the only reason human beings have sex.

We can put the reasons in the following categories; whether each is healthy or unhealthy depends on whether the parties share a focus on the category while they're having sex.

Power

If you can, at least for the moment, buy into my perspective that conquering is the second most powerful drive in humans, then you can also buy into my assertion that it can quickly bleed over into the first.

Some men see sex as a tool for domination of women or even other men. This kind of sex will usually include acts of pseudo- or even overt humiliation.

If you find yourself involved in sex that includes derogatory—or what you consider derogatory—language, then you should let him know that's not sexy talk to you. Some men have watched too many violence-laced adult films and lost sight of what is acceptable. They may even think you like insults during sex. Some of you might.

What if he's not just all talk? If he does truly domineering things in the bedroom that suggest violence on any level, make a choice right then and there: Are those actions compatible with your vision of a sex life? You have a right to say "yes;" you can even say "yes" enthusiastically if those activities are acceptable to you. But recognize that they will probably escalate in intensity. Things rarely go back to more "normal" in sex once fetishes and extremes take hold.

Entertainment

At the turn of the millennium, I was sitting with good friends who were discussing the greatest invention in history. Everyone had his or her opinion. When my time came, I said, "Birth control." I won. One could argue that birth control has made sex-as-entertainment a much cheaper form of entertainment than it had been before, particularly if you consider the potential long-term consequences of not having it. Sex for recreation is not a new idea; all you have to do is watch the History Channel's *History of Sex* series to know that. In the modern era, birth-control pioneer Margaret Sanger shared her views on the value of sex as recreation, as well as her bed, with H. G. Wells, who tried to popularize her message in the early part of the twentieth century. The central theme for them, and for you, should be this: Both parties need to see it the same way. And you have no duty to pretend you do.

That said, some women say they don't have sex for entertainment because they don't have fun with sex. Physically, they don't get it. There is no right or wrong on this one. If you think you're missing something, go find it. If not, then seek your bliss in some other areas of life.

Procreation

Couples can plan intensely when they want to have a baby and can turn sex into a mere manufacturing process. Get the cycles dialed in, do the genetic testing, take the right vitamins, be sure the employer is on board, and then have sex. Planning for stockholders' meetings is probably more fun. Again, the key is that both parties are up for this. Don't put your hands over your ears on this one: If you want to have a baby and your guy doesn't agree, go to a sperm bank. You don't want your main memory of your child's father being that he enjoyed the dinner until he got the bill.

Bonding

Caring and the desire to have sex play a role in developing the relationship. Sex implies intimacy and a continuing wish for mutual support.

Raw Need

Men have hormonal cycles, too. Athletes, particularly bodybuilders and power athletes, know this very well because many of them try to regulate those cycles artificially through the use of anabolic steroids. And the natural athletes in this group do everything they can through diet and training programs to simulate the cycles of athletes who use steroids.

The biological-clock drive is real. Women will find themselves saying "yes" to sex when they should be saying "no," because the urge to procreate is so strong that it overcomes judgment.

This is not coming from me, the male of this writing team; it's coming from Maryann, who has not only experienced the reality but also studied the physiology associated with it. As a man, I can also say that I was well aware of this because it worked to my advantage with women in their late twenties and thirties. As long as I looked strong, and like a good breeding prospect, I could appeal to women on both a conscious and a subliminal level.

Men don't have to be attracted to your psyche to be attracted to you. Until I wanted to settle down with someone, I could not have cared less about a woman's psyche.

9.

Decide:
In the Trenches

Just as each successive date should reveal more and more about your guy to you, when I interrogate someone, I am on an accelerated path to learning all about my target. In some cases, I end up knowing him better than he knows himself. I open up the control panel and see what makes him tick. I understand what kind of person he is and consciously do things to elicit the behavior I want.

Thinking back on those experiences, I have to admit I have been amazed at the goodness of some people I have met as I got to know their true natures; I have also been disgusted after scratching the surface of others and discovering they are emotionally bankrupt.

Beyond Scratching the Surface

As you continue to date a guy because you like what you see when you scratch the surface, you should experience a broadening spectrum of situations with him. Watch for inconsistencies between new quirks and traits and what you had determined was normal behavior for him. In some cases, what you saw was a veneer, and over time, veneers break down. The "true him" that you see could be a surprise: more wonderful than you could have imagined, or the nightmare on Your Street. If your dating life has always had the same elements—split a pizza, play video games, have sex, go to sleep—then it's time to add some variety. If you want a real life with him, you absolutely must explore new territory with him or you will not get to know who he really is.

It's unlikely you can give a definite answer to the following questions, among many others, until you've had continuing contact with a guy and seen him operate in a variety of venues:

- How does he treat his family?
- Are personal relationships a priority in his life?
- Is he lazy?
- Does he share your values?
- Is he stingy?
- Does he have a hidden agenda?

The framework I'll give you to answer these core questions is the seven deadly, or in some cases not-so-deadly, sins.

The Seven Sins

Greed, pride, envy, gluttony, lust, anger, and sloth show in up in everyday life. They do not start out being sins. At the root of all of them are actually traits that you *want* in a man, and as you get to know him better, you want to look for signs of them.

Greed

Greed has its roots in a desire for material wealth. When I was brand new to law school, I asked one of my professors, "What's the greatest law in history?" He replied, "The law of compound interest." What's wrong having a healthy appreciation for that? The desire to provide for a family drives a lot of people to work long hours and push for bigger and bigger payoffs. In this society, we think of that motivation as good. In contrast, many people think that if the goal itself is wealth, then all of a sudden, you've moved into the realm of greed—and that's bad.

Consider another point of view. If a man grows up in poverty and decides to do whatever it takes to make sure he never returns to it, he may appear to be greedy. Open your eyes to him as you get to know him: Does he really love money and stuff, or does he deeply fear not having them? Both of those can kill a relationship, but they don't have to. Your expectations and values establish how acceptable that is in the long term. Keep in mind that whether or not he values relationships plays in here. If he works like hell, but balances you, family, and friends, you will have more of everything.

Pride

Pride is another attribute that, in and of itself, is positive. When used to describe a deadly sin, it is consistent with Dante's

definition in *The Divine Comedy, Purgatorio*: "love of self perverted to hatred and contempt for one's neighbor." When it
gets to that point, we can all agree that pride is destructive. The
modern meaning of pride implies balance with words such as
self-respect and self-esteem, which are elements of good character and healthy personality. Both can be undermined easily by
continuously berating someone for shoddy work or treating him
badly. Pride-in-balance creates a person who strives to do well in
his chosen profession and create things he would sign his name
to. Usually, it will extend into whatever the person does and can
give the person a driving force to do things well.

Extreme pride should repel you, though. A man who boasts of
his accomplishments at the expense of others is likely to turn it on
you at some point. That kind of pride usually indicates insecurity,
anyway, rather than true competence and confidence. The great
biblical, and later literary, representation of extreme pride is John
Milton's Satan: "Better to reign in hell than serve in heaven." We
all know how that one turns out.

Vanity

My definition of vanity, which varies from the traditional one,
is pride in appearance or other natural attributes, as well as the
desire to manage others' perception of them. So, it's not an eighth
sin; it's a version of pride. Vanity and pride are two sides of the
same knife; they have a close relationship, but they aren't identi-
cal. You can have no pride and still be incredibly vain, and vice
versa. Consider the dancer in a seedy strip bar with little or no
self-esteem, but immense vanity about her appearance. Similarly,

the bodybuilder who wears a ratty old tank top to the company holiday party is vain but has little pride. In contrast, the man who knows he is the best auto mechanic around and shows up to the company party with grease under his nails may have a tremendous amount of pride but no vanity.

The core issue is what level of vanity is acceptable *to you*. Does he go out in public in holey sweats and sit on the couch letting a beer-gut hang out? That's one extreme that a lot of women will put up with because he has redeeming qualities, such as being a good provider. On the other end of the spectrum is the guy who cannot walk past a window without checking himself out because he sees himself as too gorgeous for words.

Vanity can play an insidious role in a relationship with people like that, who are "so sexy it hurts" as Right Fred Said sang in its 1991 hit *I'm Too Sexy*. It occurs when the answer to the following question is "yes": Are you too pretty for him or is he too handsome for you? Many people, regardless of how attractive they are, never seem to let this enter into the relationship equation. They believe, as I do, that no one is "too good looking" for anyone. Nevertheless, a woman who believes this may still suffer by the fact that the guy thinks she's too good looking for him. And the opposite is true. In a 2007 essay for *Time* magazine, senior editor Belinda Luscombe described the hardship of marrying outside your looks as "the last taboo" and coined the descriptor "interfacial marriage." She says she's learned to make light of comments like, "Your husband is so hot," by insisting that, "Back in Australia, I'm considered a great beauty. It's Nicole Kidman who's the hag." This is a great variation on the beauty-in-the-eye-of-the-beholder argument.

Has it ever entered your mind that you and your favorite guy are physically mismatched? In particular, a young man who dates someone who is "too pretty" for him may be very aware of it and may often wonder what she sees in him. He may tolerate a hell of a lot just to keep his trophy—and not because he loves her. If you are much more attractive than the man you are with, you have to ask yourself how healthy the relationship is. Why are you drawn to him? Is it his character? Humor? Talent? Or is it something else?

You also have to ask yourself why is he drawn to you, as well as why is he staying with you. Positive answers to the following questions could be indicators that you might be a status symbol to him, rather than part of a serious relationship:

- Does he treat you differently in public than he does in private?
- Are your opinions important, or would he rather have conversations about issues with his friends?
- Does he have pictures of you displayed in such a way that visitors to his office or home can't miss them? For example, if he has a photo of you on his desk, is it turned toward him, or does it face outward?

When I was in my early twenties, I had a serious relationship with someone I considered too pretty for me. I tolerated much more than I should have from her and even fell in love with her. One morning, after the relationship had soured, one of my fellow soldiers saw this woman as she dropped me off at the office and remarked, "She's beautiful. I can see why you are drawn to her."

My answer was, "Yeah, but if someone gave you a Lamborghini and parked it on your foot, what would you do to get it off?"

If you are involved with a man you feel is too good looking for you, you need to determine if he feels the same way. Sometimes looks genuinely don't matter, but sometimes a good-looking man or woman wants someone he feels is less attractive because he or she knows the other will tolerate more. That is a recipe for abuse. If he treats you harshly, as though you are less important than he is, then you know the relationship is not healthy. Another bad sign is keeping the relationship so private that you never see any of his friends.

Envy

Envy and shoes. Envy and cars. Envy and education. Envy and the ability to meditate like a guru. Envy is about wanting what someone else has. Envy is what the entire luxury retailing industry depends on, for example. In his book, *Crossing Fifth Avenue to Bergdorf Goodman,* Ira Neimark captures in a simple phrase what he aimed to do—and succeeded in doing—when he became Bergdorf Goodman's CEO: He transformed an "old, dull, expensive, and intimidating store" into a "young, exciting, expensive, and intimidating store." That premise played successfully on envy as a normal, entrenched characteristic of people who want to improve themselves. Does that sound so bad?

Our culture revolves around wanting to be a millionaire or an American idol. We emulate those at the top of pop culture to raise ourselves up the ladder. We are a country of people who came here for the opportunity. That kind of envy is good.

If it were not for a healthy amount of envy, many people would not find the incentive to get better jobs, create opportunities for their kids to have great educations, and find the resources to take you to Hawaii for your first anniversary. Envy goes bad when we want more than we can afford or have the capability to produce. Balance keeps us from getting the big house that we cannot afford to furnish. Or the car we cannot afford to insure.

Envy also drives our desire for more in every situation. There are men and women who look at their friends' partners, girlfriends, and wives and cannot be happy until they have them. They must acquire the prize, even at the cost of a friendship. When you are dating someone and his friend calls you, think about what might be going on. Don't be naïve. Some men are never satisfied with the woman they are with; they change women like cars, trading up to the latest model. In some cases, this has little to do with sexual desire and a lot to do with status. The question dividing good from bad is this: "Will my acquiring this hurt anyone?"

Gluttony

Gluttony is about extravagance; you consume more than you need. Indulging yourself is not necessarily bad. Giving yourself a treat—even the occasional binge, I'd argue—is not bad. It's just that if you repeat it over and over, the behavior is harmful to you and probably other people, too. It's in that repetition that gluttony becomes a sin. Indulging yourself occasionally as a reward, a celebration, or an aberration is just gluttony as a form of normal human pleasure.

What do you call someone who never succumbs to gluttony? Someone who has control issues. He never has an extra bite of dessert. He never has an extra glass of wine with dinner. He never dances until dawn when he has to go work the next day. It's normal human behavior to go overboard every once in a while. It's not normal to beat yourself up for it every time it happens.

When you first meet a man and he says, "I never drink alcohol," find out why. Maybe his father was an alcoholic, or maybe he was. Or maybe he had a bad experience with it as young man and just isn't interested. There's nothing wrong with any of those things, but you have a right to be curious.

Lust

Lust is one of those things you can't live without but that you might have problems living with. The deadly-sin definition talks about inordinate cravings for physical pleasures. Okay, define "inordinate." Any man who wants to have sex with every woman he has contact with has serious psychological issues that go beyond lust. But what if a couple has such great enjoyment in having sex with each other than they have (ostensibly) unreasonable cravings for each other? And let's complicate this scenario by saying that these two people are married? So, in that situation, is lust bad?

If you are in a relationship in which one or both of you have absolutely no desire for a physical connection—then I suggest you move on. We are all shaved apes, animals with rituals of civilization, but nonetheless, animals.

Anger

Anger, in the traditional definition of "bad," entails a rejection of love in favor of rage. Well, as someone who has fought for American principles, I would affirm that a certain amount of anger keeps you free. Not only that, but a certain amount of anger keeps your relationships normal. At the crux of this assertion is that the expression of anger need not be devoid of respect.

Every relationship involves entitlements, and they're extremely important in determining whether or not a relationship will endure. Whether the subject is a car loan or day care, or the relationship is priest-to-confessor or husband-to-wife, all involve entitlements. Some are legally defined, or expressed specifically in conversation, while others are simply implied.

Probably the most complex of these is the romantic relationship, which commonly involves all three. What happens when one of these entitlements is violated? Do we have the right to be angry? To discuss it passionately?

Your arguing with a man about an entitlement will set expectations about "what next." Or you can just let him get away with whatever you perceived as a violation of your rights. Becoming a shrew is the extreme.

Why do anger, and the associated activity of argument, have such ugly connotations? Does the phrase "legal argument" disturb you? When a coach argues an umpire's call, is that a "sin?" If someone steals your purse and your boyfriend angrily chases him down the street to reclaim it, should you be disappointed because he actually cared about reclaiming your material possessions? These examples point to channeling anger constructively, and if you can do that, then anger has the potential to be a positive force.

The manifestations of anger can, of course, cause anxiety, pain, and even death. Many people perceive explosive anger as intrinsically bad. They recoil at a shout or a crash or thud that's been caused by someone who's angry. If you are one of those people, you may be with a guy who literally makes you sick with his expressions of anger. Do you still want to be with him every day if that never changes?

Going into a relationship with someone who is explosive, and making him feel guilty for those overt demonstrations of anger, may make him suppress those outbursts, but the anger is still there. Ask yourself whether or not you are trying to bridle the wild horse. Those little intermittent explosions might mean the issue is closed when the outburst ends. I can say this with authority because that's what happens with me. After an initial reaction, I am over it and it is forgotten.

Men I know who do not show anger like this—like a quick burst of a geyser—have told me they wish they could because they have found that containing anger causes them to hold a grudge. Both have positives and negatives and you need to know which works for you.

Note well: People who never show anger are the most dangerous people.

Sloth

Sloth means that a person is not willing to give of himself to grow or develop—whether physically, spiritually, emotionally, or intellectually. In terms of relationships, it means he holds back. Sounds as though there's nothing positive about it, but it's not a death sentence for a relationship. Do you find him modeling your behavior, such as going for walks with you and helping to do the dishes? Is there any friend he respects who gets him excited about reading books or going to the gym? There's hope.

Does he sleep ten hours a day or seem to drag himself through activities? Maybe there's more than just sloth at work here. He could suffer from depression, chronic fatigue syndrome, or some other illness.

As you date, you will get the opportunity to spend time with him in the presence of his family and friends. Think about how each of these seven deadly sins (plus vanity) plays into his interaction with them. On the following pages are charts of positive and negative indicators associated with the seven in each situation, one chart for family and one chart for friends. Create your own. If the relationship grows, you will become a unique creature—the family he *chose*. You will likely see a blending of these behaviors in how he treats you.

Take each of the "sins" and see how it relates to the questions that I posed at the introduction to this section. Build your own charts out of your answers to the questions.

How Does He Treat His Family?

When you're dating seriously, your ultimate goal is to be part of that person's family. So if your guy treats his family harshly or with a lack of concern, how will he treat you when you're his family? Most normal families have periodic turbulence in their relationships, so I'm not talking about judging his behavior on the basis of an isolated remark or incident. Watch for patterns. Does he always refer to his sister as an idiot? Does he always roll his eyes when he talks to his mother on the phone? Does he make fun of his father's fat belly at every opportunity? All of us have baggage with family, but unkindness to family is a bad sign.

This guy might be jovial with the rest of the world and cut his friends a break when they do offensive things. When it comes to his family, though, the judgmental part of him flares up. You see a different person—a guy you don't like very much. Consider that it might be the guy you would see every day if you were married to him.

Are Personal Relationships a Priority in His Life?

A man can make plenty of time for you and his buddies and still not consider relationships a priority in his life. He might make time for you because of the sex, and he might spend plenty of time with his buddies because of the poker. Conversely, a guy who appears to be a workaholic may drop everything when his friend has surgery and needs a helping hand. The only way you will know is to watch for patterns.

Another aspect of the question relates to bandwidth. A guy who tries to maintain relationships because they have a central role in his life may not give you the attention you want upfront. Dating you simply does not represent a relationship to him—at least not yet. If you see the signs that he values his friends and family, then just give him time. He'll either shift toward giving you more focus, and maybe spending a little less time with his

SIN	NEGATIVE INDICATORS WITH FAMILY	POSITIVE INDICATORS WITH FAMILY
Sloth	Mom, sis, and other members of the family wait on him hand and foot	Relaxes, sits, and listens to family
Greed	Overly concerned about parents' spending	Working extra hours so he can be giving and caring with parents even if they make bad money decisions
Pride	Indignant when questioned, as though he always knows more than they do/Ashamed to show you his family; always apologizing for them	Celebrating achievements with them, his and theirs/Projecting self-esteem without any sense of an I'm-too-good-for-you attitude
Vanity	Puts down their appearance, especially his father's physique (that's probably where he's headed!)	Complimentary of his mother's earrings or dad's tie, even if they are the only things on them he likes
Envy	Sibling rivalry to the extreme	Wants to model them, such as go to same college; doctors and lawyers run in families for a reason—family tradition of excellence
Gluttony	Overeats at mother's house; goes overboard with everything because it's there and he's not paying for it	Able to party hearty with his family at weddings, birthday bashes, etc.
Lust	*Not applicable, except with hillbillies*	
Anger	If anyone can push a person's buttons, it's family, but that is not an invitation to be disrespectful with them	Animated disapproval, while showing respect

SIN	NEGATIVE INDICATORS WITH FRIENDS	POSITIVE INDICATORS WITH FRIENDS
Sloth	Rather than going anywhere, he tells people to come over—and bring something/Knows nothing about his friends, because he makes no emotional investment; friends are just bodies in his life	Relaxes; sits and listens to friends—not "on" all the time
Greed	Chooses friends for what they can provide/Never pays for anything; tries to avoid the check	Wants the best of everything, but is sensitive to others' strained resources—invites them over for dinner instead of going out
Pride	Condescending; belittles others	Acknowledging value (of relationship, as well as contribution) person brings to the world
Vanity	Only hangs out with beautiful people, or only hangs out with people who are less attractive so he appears more attractive	Gives compliments that help bolster others' self-image so they never feel less-than
Envy	Minimizes accomplishment of friends	Asks for pointers to improve his game, their finances, etc.
Gluttony	Drinks too much, eats too much, smokes too much	Not afraid to enjoy the company of friends to the fullest
Lust	Constantly hitting on women he shouldn't be hitting on/Women can't be friends, they are all possible lovers	Flirting with a female friend without intention, making a woman feel better about her attractiveness without hitting on her
Anger	Bullying; dominates friends so they are afraid to say anything to him	Engages in animated disagreement aimed at a resolution, shows respect

buddies, or start to pull away. The latter situation is often a real heartbreaker because you can see that he cares about relationships, but he just doesn't see having one with you. Move on.

Is He Lazy?

Some people are born waiting to retire. They define "accomplishment" as not having to do anything they don't want to do and still having what they need to live. Other people define "accomplishment" in terms of dollars, or good-looking children, or advanced degrees. Your definition of "accomplishment" is key to answering the question, "Is he lazy?" Try to take an objective look at him by putting him into one of these categories:

- **High energy, low activity:** I know a woman who regularly stays up until three o'clock in the morning and visits chat rooms on the Internet. Nearly all night, she's up drinking soda and eating candy as she types messages to strangers. She's the epitome of the high-energy, low activity person.
- **High activity, low energy:** You can be born a low-energy person, or turn into one because of disease, for example, and yet use your time productively. It doesn't mean you literally have to make things; the result of high energy doesn't have to be tangible. A nun in a cloister who prays all day can be high activity and low energy.
- **High energy, high activity:** Professional athletes would commonly fit into this category. When they retire, then all bets are off.

- **Low energy, low activity:** I wouldn't want to say this definitively, but someone who fits this profile might be suffering from a debilitating physical or mental illness.

At this point, you might conclude that the guy isn't lazy at all but that you are discounting what he considers accomplishment. As long as you hold onto that judgment, your relationship is on shaky ground.

Does He Share Your Values?

This builds on the concept of discounting the other person's views. A guy can disagree with you on religion, politics, and money, but if his passion or arrogance prevents him from having a respectful conversation about them with you, then you are with the wrong guy.

That's why you need to engage in conversation on these topics early in a relationship. Find out before it's too late whether or not just talking about them is a divisive exercise.

Look in the mirror, too. If you don't understand money, then you will be disconnected from someone who is driven by it. If he has deeply held religious beliefs that you feel are bogus, then he will either try to convert you or expend a lot of energy feeling sorry for you. Do not back off from these differences; be certain how well, or poorly, you talk about them.

If you disagree profoundly on the appropriate way to express religious beliefs, you might be able to talk through that one. But if your situation is belief versus nonbelief in God and an afterlife, that is a meaningful enough conflict to cause a split. If you firmly believe in paradise and you're counting on spending the rest of eternity with the man you love, but he thinks that death puts an end to every bit of you, your visions of the future might differ too radically to be reconciled.

Is He Stingy?

Stingy comes in different flavors: financial, emotional, spiritual, physical, and on and on. It can come from pure selfishness, but many times, "stingy" has roots in childhood poverty (again, that can come in many flavors), frugality cultivated by parents, or as a rebellion against parental behavior and values.

When I was a little kid—just five or six—I had very few books, but they were my favorite possessions. My mother knew that giving me a book, and reading to me, made me happy. I would always put my books high on a shelf so that other kids would keep their hands off them. I knew that, if I put them where kids with dirty hands and crayons could get to them, that they would destroy my favorite things. Later on, I found myself doing that with other possessions that I valued, and I consciously corrected the behavior. I realized that, in a pronounced way, I was being stingy with certain things and that communicated a lack of trust to people in my life.

Some people are in a state of arrested development when it comes to things they value—or to a piece of their heart. They are habitually stingy. If this is just a habit, it can be broken. But if the root is mistrust because someone broke their toys or their heart, then it is possible that the behavior will not change—or it will take a long time. Are you willing to wait?

Does He Have a Hidden Agenda?

For purposes of discussion here, I'm defining *hidden agenda* as an ulterior motive, rather than something that's part of his unconscious or subconscious. An example of the latter would be that, without even realizing it, he's dating you because he thinks his family would accept you. An example of a hidden agenda is his desire to have you support him so he can focus on writing a science-fiction novel.

The hidden agenda has a finite lifespan: If I get her to do X, then I will get Y. To follow that logic along, "And when I get Y, I can move on to someone, or something, else."

A high-profile example is the marriage of author Terry McMillan and gigolo Jonathan Plummer.

"It was devastating to discover that a relationship I had publicized to the world as life-affirming and built on mutual love was actually based on deceit." With these words to the Contra Costa (California) Superior Court, Terry McMillan officially called her husband a liar. Her husband forgot to mention that he was gay during the romantic encounters that led to *How Stella Got Her Groove Back*. Can you just hear him now? "Honey, it slipped my mind!" (Or whatever idiom they use in Jamaica.)

Could Terry have caught that scoundrel before the happy island romance turned into a disputed prenup? Here are nine tips I would have given Terry—tips I would give any woman—to avoid being sucked into a relationship with a hidden agenda. They apply across the board, regardless of what the agenda is:

1. Do not give him outs when you ask questions just because you want to hear a particular response. These are the leading questions covered in Chapter 6. During a trial, it's the kind of question that the opposing attorney hears and jumps to her feet with, "Objection, your honor! Leading the witness."

2. When he looks into your eyes, are his eyes a little rounder than when he's in casual conversation with the guys? It's a sign that he really is attracted to you. Another is that his cheeks have a bit more color and his lips seem fuller. (Yes, you can detect the change on someone with dark skin. Humans evolved in such a way that our eyes are sensitive to subtle changes in skin tone. You just have to pay attention.) The same blood flow we need for erections goes to other fleshy mucous membranes in our bodies. These responses to sexual arousal are involuntary and universal. If you see these signs, you have no guarantee that he's on the level—he might still have a hidden agenda—but at least you know that his attraction to you is genuine.

3. Do you see those signs when he's around another woman—or a man? Now there's a sign of trouble!

4. Does he go out of his way to agree with you—even about silly things? If a man is trying to get you in bed (or get your money) or is simply desperate for companionship, he may even agree to lots of things that are not true for him.

5. Does he leak signs of stress when you bring up certain topics, like his background or relationships? These would include adaptors, discussed in Chapter 2, as well as stronger signals

such as an eye twitch. For most people, lying creates some level of stress. (See Chapter 7 for more information on detecting and breaking a liar.)

6. Does he answer questions about certain topics in a way that's different from his normal tone and cadence? For example, when you ask about his last serious relationship, does his response seem rehearsed? Or maybe vague and staccato when you're used to him describing things in fluid detail? Could be he's hiding something.

7. Does he keep turning the conversation back to you, so you realize you are finding out almost nothing about him? Or does he talk *at* you, as described in Chapter 4, when he talks about himself, so you have no good opening to have a dialogue about him?

8. Anyone who talks in grandiose terms about his "love," which "knows no limits" blah, blah, blah, is in love with being in love. That is bound for failure, too.

9. Trust your intuition. Even if he passes the tests of body language, as well as vocal and verbal communication, your gut might tell you something is wrong. You're a woman. You have a giant corpus collosum, compared to a man's, and that allows you to shuttle information between your left brain and right brain, between the side that handles complex problems (the "logic" side) and the other that has a more panoramic view of a situation (the "creative" side). Your intuition is real.

10.

Decide: Does He Stay or Does He Go?

Your basic question in deciding whether or not to continue a relationship is this: Does he violate my entitlements? When we enter into most types of relationships that we expect to be enduring, we set clear expectations. To start a new job, buy a car, or rent an apartment, both parties involved expect that the details of the agreement will be clear. In many of these cases, of course, we have little choice; we are dealing with non-negotiable, boilerplate contracts. Oddly enough, maybe that learned behavior has something to do with why we seldom do a good job of discussing entitlement in relationships.

The Importance of Entitlements

Every relationship has entitlements embedded in it. Regardless of what you call them, entitlements involve respect for people and things that matter to you. They are vital elements in your definition of quality of life and, therefore, in the quality of your relationship. The less you expect from life and from relationships, the fewer hard-and-fast entitlements you will have.

Everyone has certain entitlements, and when a man violates yours, or you violate his, then you will feel offended. You might get angry, or you might even consider the violation a deal-breaker and end the relationship. The same holds true for him.

In 1990, when I had daily involvement with the SERE (Survival, Evasion, Resistance, Escape) school, I was living with a British girl who did not know—because I couldn't let her know—precisely what I did all day at work. After hours of putting our soldiers through psychological and physical hardships as part of their training, I'd come home to her cavalier question, "How was your day at the office, dear?" Her expectation was that, as an intelligence professional, I sat around and analyzed things all day at my desk. If I'd stayed with her, imagine how she would have felt if I'd gotten a call at 3 A.M. and heard the order, "Be here in thirty minutes," and then disappeared for a few weeks. Her presumed entitlement that I would come home every day after work would be seriously violated.

Entitlements can be spoken or implied, and in this case, it was implied. I never promised to come home every day after work. That would not mitigate the violation. In the dating stages, men and women do this all time by cheating on the other person and then arguing, "I never *said* I'd be faithful to you!" Maybe not, but if you've been seeing someone very steadily for a few months, wouldn't you think that the other person might have developed a sense of entitlement that you wouldn't sleep around?

There are two types of entitlements: stated, in which someone explicitly states what she expects, and implied, in which someone has expectations for something that has not been concretely stated or established. As you consider the two types of entitlements and how violations of them can be deal-breakers, keep in mind that what is frivolous to one person may be serious to another.

Clear Expectations—Stated Entitlements

You have had conversations specifically about these topics and come to an agreement. They can be serious matters, such as fidelity, or ostensibly minor things, such as "I promise I'll never use your razor to shave my legs."

Every couple should talk about religion, sex, and politics early on, and they should do it again after the two of you feel comfortable enough with each other to stop holding back about your opinions. Some very important value statements should surface in these discussions, and those value statements will help you articulate key expectations.

Inferred Expectations—Implied Entitlements

At least one of you thinks that it's natural to expect that these entitlements will be honored. Typical expectations would include entitlements such as these: You won't steal from me. You won't throw my dog down the trash chute. You will say "Thank you" when I feed you. Other, slightly more unusual ones would be that you don't expect someone who works at the post office to disappear for a week. If you're in a relationship with a Secret Service agent, however, his sudden departure might not make you happy, but it shouldn't necessarily rattle your sense of entitlement.

And then there are the issues you thought you had discussed, but it turns out only one of you thought so. For example, maybe you've talked about splitting the bill when you go to a restaurant and you agree that, for the time being at least, that's how you'd like to do it. But whenever he comes over to your house, he feels free to raid the fridge, drink your wine, and dip into your cookie jar—and never brings anything over.

In your mind, that's an abuse of your resources, which you thought you'd addressed by talking about splitting the cost of meals. From his perspective, it's possible that he looks at your apartment as his other home, so he'll behave at your place just like he does at his mom's. Not a good sign in this case.

Or is it? You may be the one with entitlement issues here if he thinks that, based on your behavior, your home is his home and that you simply prefer to split the cost of food in public. Address an issue like this directly. When his head is in the fridge, ask him if he could stop by the store next time he's on the way over and pick up another bottle of juice. Don't assume you've established an expectation about a little thing like this; he simply may not get it.

"Common entitlements" is an oxymoron. Every person, and every couple, has a set of expectations that reflect background, education, values, the opinions of friends, what pop psychologists say is important, and just plain weird stuff. That said, entitlements that commonly case trouble when violated fall into the following categories.

Sex

The first thing to consider when it comes to sex and entitlement is the issue of fidelity. We know well from the maelstrom that nearly ended Bill Clinton's presidency prematurely that the definition of fidelity might not be the same for everyone. How do you define it? How do you define it as a couple? Some women go ballistic at the thought of their guy getting a lap dance from a stripper, whereas other women find it a normal, noninvasive activity that he can enjoy freely. I knew a young couple who had clear entitlement about this. She told him if she found out that he had been to a strip bar, then she would have him killed. They have long since been divorced.

Another point of contention could be how frequently you or your partner believes you are entitled to sex. If you aren't willing to have sex every time you see each other, are you violating his entitlement? Is he violating your expectation that, at least occasionally, you want to go to sleep without someone having an orgasm?

Next, of course, is the issue of the type of sex each person in a relationship believes he or she is entitled to. I'm not telling you anything you don't know here. Some men actually think that they have a right to change positions, receive oral sex (maybe even give it), and do other variations on a theme once you've been together a while. And for some women, if they don't get some variety, then *their* entitlements have been violated.

Then there is an entitlement that usually causes the most issue for the female set: the ability to climax. You have the right to an orgasm. This entitlement does not have to be discussed at length, but it may have to be reinforced. Regardless of whether you "just" want to procreate, or you "just" want to have a good time, you should not feel timid about having fun.

Security

One point to consider when it comes to entitlement and security is emotions. The range of emotional expressions from love to hate can involve everything from the tenderest display of caring to hateful outbursts. Maybe you feel you have a right not to be exposed to either extreme, or you feel that only expressions toward the love side of the scale are acceptable. Commonly, no matter what you and he have agreed to regarding how emotion gets vented, all bets are off when people are angry, and you might be dealing with a double whammy here because the cause of the anger is likely a violation of an entitlement. My anger is explosive, but then it's over quickly and the matter is history. Other people seethe with anger and carry grudges, but they feel that not exploding gave them control. In some families, maintaining that control in expected under all circumstances.

Another important factor in the security/entitlement equation is the value of truth. The security of knowing that the person you're with tells you the truth habitually is one of those universal, implied rights that gets violated in two ways. The obvious one is lying. The counterpart to it is radical honesty. Sometimes honesty is a weapon. Someone who is overly honest may be toying with you by remarking negatively about your weight, for example, when you are well aware of the fact that you've gained a few pounds and are trying to take it off.

Tolerance for change also plays a role when considering someone's sense of entitlement when it comes to security. Protecting the status quo dominates some people's sense of security. They have limited or no tolerance for a new restaurant or position in bed, much less the dramatic change of raising a child, changing jobs, or moving to a different city. A person in military service or in any other profession that involves lots of moving around should never marry a person like this, although it happens all the time and heads toward divorce almost from day one.

Resources

The first category of resources is financial. Address this issue openly because a lot of relationships break up over it. The different flavors of financial entitlements include these approaches to handling money: priority versus necessary evil, generosity versus frugality, joint checking versus separation of funds, and financial partner versus provider.

A man or woman driven to make money has inferred entitlements that reflect the priority status of money. Being late for dinner because of a meeting or missing a family event to finalize a deal is appropriate behavior. On the other hand, a person who eschews money because "it's the root of all evil" might feel that he or she has the right to interrupt an important meeting with an "urgent" call that turns out to concern something like the death of a rosebush.

Some people see generosity as a fundamental virtue. Whether it relates to a church alliance or to a favorite charity, the mentality of giving dominates their monetary planning and decisions. This may also surface in the desire to tip wait staff or housekeepers in a hotel. Some people, because of what they've gone through to make a decent living, have extreme sensitivity to the needs of service personnel and tip extremely well. On the other hand, "Watch the pennies and the dollars will take care of themselves" has been a positive mantra for many people who don't see generosity as a reasonable default behavior.

The root of a decision to have joint or separate checking accounts is usually either parental or personal experience. Do not force a joint-checking arrangement if everything in your background tells you it's doomed to failure. Try to a compromise like "his, mine, and ours." I know of a couple, both successful architects, who had separate accounts as well as a "play account." It didn't have much money in it, but it was something that either one could draw down freely as long as the money was used for something that both of them could enjoy.

The concept of "provider" survives, despite what popular media might lead you to believe. Maryann has a friend whose parents raised her to have very old-fashioned expectations about money. In her life, the man in a relationship, whether it's a first date or a marriage, has the responsibility to ante up. Her responsibilities are to maintain a perfect weight, clear complexion, beautiful wardrobe—you get the picture. She is not shallow, nor does she deceive the men she is with. That's her entitlement, and a man can either take it or leave it, but there is no excuse for his accepting it on the first date, and then shifting behavior on the fourth. His entitlement in this situation is information about what she expects. If someone pays for the first date, does he understand that she expects him to pay for all the others? If not, I call that taking someone for granted.

Time is your most valuable resource, so if you do not have rules about it with your dates or your partner, you are cheating yourself. You are entitled to a hot bath—alone—or a night out with your sorority sisters. Don't just throw your time around in response to everyone else's demands, and be careful not to expect that your guy will drop everything and make time for you. Just like money, you have to talk about the allocation of this resource and be very specific about your expectations. When you are consistently late by fifteen to thirty minutes, ask yourself the question: Is he entitled to something here? And you may think you're flexible about time, but when he shows up two hours late for a date for which you'd dressed up, done your nails and makeup, and gotten a special haircut, you will feel violated, and he should know it.

Your personal contacts are a resource that you do not have to share. Let's say you're best friend is an attorney, and your boyfriend just got a DUI citation. He wants free legal advice, so he calls your friend, who feels obligated to help. Somebody needs to serve double jail time! Another one I've seen that contributed substantially to a breakup was the boyfriend in network marketing who tried corral all of his girlfriend's pals into his various sure-thing businesses. If you or the friends offer the help and he takes it, that's a different story. The part that is a violation is being taken for granted, as well as his using your contacts as his resource.

Social

Level of activity can have a considerable role in your social entitlements. When you first date someone, you typically do something other than sitting at home, watching television or playing video games. However, one of you might long for the day when that's all you do, while the other one wants to keep going to clubs and movies and the bowling alley. Your mismatched expectations about level of activity will cause friction on a regular basis. Ultimately, this is what can drive one of the partners—usually the one who wants to go out—to seek the company of someone who enjoys the dating activities.

Undoubtedly, some of the things you used to do will not fit a different relationship, either. If you've spent a lot of time in bars because you liked it, that pastime may not play well with a more established relationship. Many marriages split because rituals from the past are so deeply embedded that one partner loses sight of the other person's entitlements. When he's presented with the same old stimulus, he responds the same old way.

The desire to host or not to host can also be a deal-breaker. Hospitality is not a gift that everyone has. For those who don't, the idea of hosting a dinner party, for example, could cause a nervous breakdown. If one of you takes enormous pleasure in having people over and the other hates the thought, you may have an irreconcilable difference.

Family

You can look at these related entitlements in terms of past, present, and future.

Heritage is a sensitive issue for many people, mostly because they feel as though people outside of it cannot fully appreciate it. The sense of entitlement that a person associates with his or her family background needs to be articulated. You can't just guess that your guy feels persecuted because of his color, or that he understands how deeply important the family tartan and annual Highland Games are to you. Heritage is a mirror of any issue someone holds sacred. The idea that something is very important to you and he would trivialize it is a guarantee for failure.

In terms of the present, here's a top deal-breaker for lots of people we talked with: "Disrespecting my family." You shouldn't have to tell the person you're dating that you expect him to show respect to your family—right? Right. If you feel you have to articulate that, then someone is way off base in this relationship. Many people may criticize their own families, but that's not an invitation for outsiders to join in. He may call his father a dumb fat oaf, but remember: The apple often falls close to the tree. What happens when he wakes up and realizes he is a dumb fat (or thin) oaf? If you chimed in with similar criticism of Dad, he might wake up on that day of realization and think, "That's what she thinks of me."

And when it comes to the future, be clear about this. Very clear. Your greatest desire may be to have and raise children. With him. That does not mean that you have an entitlement to get pregnant—unless you've discussed this beforehand. There is also the scenario in which you do not want children, but you do get pregnant. Here, I'm not talking about someone you had one date with but someone you've been seeing for a while. You do not have the entitlement to eliminate the pregnancy without informing him—unless you discussed this beforehand. Yes, you have the legal right, but that is *not* the same as an entitlement within a relationship. Two people; two sets of expectations. Honor that.

Regardless of whether children ever become an issue between you, if you move into a committed relationship, you become each other's family, and you're likely to revert to behaviors you use with your blood relatives. He might feel he's entitled to leave the room and find a quiet space when an argument erupts; you might feel you're entitled to a no-holds-barred fight just like the ones you used to have with your brothers and sisters. The first time something like that happens, you need to establish a new entitlement for your new family.

Career

Career issues involve primarily identity and goals. For some people, their career describes who they are, not merely what they do. Look beyond the obvious to see if that applies to him or to you. It isn't just professionals like doctors, teachers, writers, and actors who have a right to be passionate about their careers and link them to their identities. A guy who sells real estate may see his mission as finding homes for people, not just houses. A florist may consider herself an artist, bringing beauty to the world through living art. A deal-breaker for someone like that is trivializing his career or suggesting he's not that good at it. Here's another offense: competing with the career for his time and attention. For example, it would be mistake to buy tickets for playoff games the week before a writer's book is due to the publisher.

The same entitlements can apply to a hobby, too. Maybe you work Monday through Friday at a job you hate, but it supports your weekends of skydiving. So when someone new in your life asks, "What do you do?" you don't say, "Wait tables," you reply,

"I'm a skydiver." And when you finally decide what you want to be when you grow up, the last thing you need is someone slinging discouragement at you as you try to achieve your goal. You feel as though you have a right to expect the other person in your relationship to find ways to be supportive. I know of a marriage in which this became a central, divisive issue; the couple is now divorced.

The following chart indicates how a couple might rank violations of both stated and implied entitlements in terms of importance.

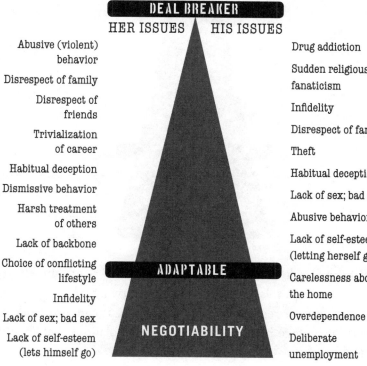

DEAL BREAKER

HER ISSUES   HIS ISSUES

ADAPTABLE

NEGOTIABILITY

HER ISSUES	HIS ISSUES
Abusive (violent) behavior	Drug addiction
Disrespect of family	Sudden religious fanaticism
Disrespect of friends	Infidelity
Trivialization of career	Disrespect of family
Habitual deception	Theft
Dismissive behavior	Habitual deception
Harsh treatment of others	Lack of sex; bad sex
Lack of backbone	Abusive behavior
Choice of conflicting lifestyle	Lack of self-esteem (letting herself go)
Infidelity	Carelessness about the home
Lack of sex; bad sex	Overdependence
Lack of self-esteem (lets himself go)	Deliberate unemployment

Now, I suggest you create a chart like this consciously—together—as you go through the process of deciding whether or not the guy you've been dating is a keeper.

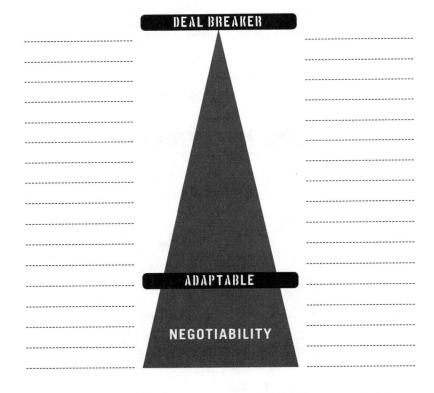

Where does love fit in all of this? Love can work to your advantage in keeping a relationship together by driving you to be more generous in your responses to his violations. It can also work to your disadvantage by distracting you from violations that should be deal-breakers.

Arranged marriages sound like a horrible idea to most people, but the positive aspect of them is that they involve matched expectations. Entitlements are clear. They may have been codified by religion, culture, and family. The couple has nothing to say about them, but they at least they know where they stand.

On the other hand, a modern marriage centered on love and/ or passion often involves mismatched expectations. Both people make sweeping assumptions about entitlements, but it isn't until their assumptions cause arguments that they even realize the problem. Use the information in this chapter to help avoid that debacle.

Productive Versus Corrosive Arguing

You can understand something intellectually and yet emotionally override it. Countering that emotional impulse is sometimes difficult—and not countering it will lead to an argument. This happens all the time when people disagree about entitlements, even the ones that are not anywhere near deal-breakers. For example, one of my female friends has very particular ways of handling kitchen implements. It used to be that, if she saw her husband use the "wrong" knife to cut something, she went little nuts. After a few stupid arguments, she learned to say simply, "Honey, just indulge me. Please don't use my filet knife to chop onions." Hearing that, it's incumbent on him to oblige, even though it doesn't make a damned bit of sense to him. Look at it from his perspective: At least he is not using the filet knife as a screwdriver. Hammering out the details in a relationship is like negotiating a contract. The kitchen-implements example shows a productive approach to a disagreement, rather than one that's corrosive.

A lot of women will not assert themselves out of fear of wrecking the deal. The push their emotional responses to a man's actions down inside and bite their tongues when they see him use the wrong knife or put a glass of cold water on a nice wooden table. Men tend to get ticked off and have little explosions on the spot.

The big problem with suppressing the anger is that it will likely surface later, either at an inappropriate time or in a way that is way out proportion for the new circumstance that has triggered it. Here's the solution:

CLARIFY YOUR EXPECTATIONS. State them outright, and do not just assume that implying them through example or analogy or a bunch of meaningful stories is going to get the message across.

WORK THOUGH WHAT IS AN ACCEPTABLE EXPECTATION AND WHAT IS BEYOND REASONABLE. Do you really want to break up over when to use a filet knife? If you're a professional chef, maybe you do. Find a central ground: If the knife is not negotiable, then move on to someone who appreciates knives.

SET BOUNDARIES. In a respectful tone, remind him what your stated expectations are when he inadvertently (or heaven forbid, deliberately) violates them.

LEAVE HIM IF HE VIOLATES THEM OVER AND OVER AGAIN. Even if he has what he considers "a good reason," he hasn't respected your emotional investment in the expectation. In this case, I am talking about the deal breakers only and not the little things.

Commonly, men don't intentionally build an argument on emotion. So when emotion creeps in and shapes the argument, that's powerful. Let's say you and your boyfriend are discussing gang warfare in a major urban area, and you say, "I feel that these kids would not be fighting each other if they could count on a decent education, three meals a day, and health care." He comes back with, "What are you, stupid? Any fool can see . . ." then you have a man arguing in an emotional state, even though logic drives his behavior. Despite the fact that he's armed with good information, calling you stupid and implying you're a fool are elements not of an intellectual exercise but an emotional one. No one wins this argument if it keeps heading in this direction, and worse yet, no one learns from this argument. It quickly becomes a matter of who can yell the loudest.

Recognize that no two people ever believe exactly the same thing. You can have a good, healthy argument if you address topics that are meaningful enough so that you have a vested interest in learning to agree to disagree. A disagreement over who should be president is not a reason to split up; you should be able to argue it vigorously, but then leave it alone.

11.

Decide: Red Alerts

In an interrogation setting, I have to decide whether the person I am dealing with is genuine or pretending to be something else to make himself less attractive to me. In your dating life, you have the opposite confusion. A guy may act like a son of a bitch to attract you.

The problem lies in knowing whether the act is authentic for the guy, or whether it's just a role adopted to get you to notice him. All people play multiple roles. It's normal that a person is not exactly the same in interactions with his mother as he is with his boss. Red flags go up when one role seems dramatically different from other. The point at which you should start to be concerned is when the guy is Jekyll and Hyde from day to day. The abusive boyfriend who slaps you and then displays true guilt as he begs for forgiveness through his tears is no better for you than the guy who routinely beats you and tells you that you deserve it. Neither one deserves your pity or your unwavering loyalty.

This is a short list of men with the potential to be that Jekyll-Hyde monster.

NARCISSISTS
The Marshmallow Center Is Depression

After a great deal of exposure to narcissists, I developed my own definition of their problem: Narcissism is a bridge between self-loathing and insecurity accompanied by self-aggrandizing behavior. A psychologist friend of mine says, "Scratch a narcissist and you find depression." We agree that depression often has its roots in self-loathing.

The narcissist is trying to live up to a model he can't touch, to be bigger than he is as a way of hiding internal issues. Saddam Hussein is an example. Time and again, I've seen the source as the narcissist either trying to better his father's image or to at least live up to it. The father may not have done anything to cause this, other than live a successful life.

Your challenge in having a relationship with a narcissist is that you only have value in terms of him—you have no value, except how you impact his life. Things like your career, your family, and your pets all have to have value in his life in order for you to matter to him.

If you make him look bad, he's likely to lash out. He's already insecure. Hit his soft spots, and he will feel the need to retaliate.

MOOD SWINGERS
Do You Want It to Be Two for the Seesaw?

The passion that comes with the mania may attract you, but the inevitable drop to the void could take you to hell.

If you are dealing with a man with an illness, then what it comes down to is how responsibly the person handles it. I am *not* one of those people who thinks that a diagnosis of mental illness means that you have to run to a pharmacist. But I am someone who recognizes that, whatever illness you have, you can't ignore it and hope it will go away.

Your mood swinger may not be mentally ill, however. Maybe he's just a person of extremes who gets consumed with the desire to write a novel in eight days, or to live in the garage until he finishes building his model airplane. Lots of women have lived happily ever after with men like that. Then again, lots of women have left them without the men even noticing for week.

If you meet someone in a manically productive state and he thrills you, energizes you, and sucks you into his whirlwind life, just don't make any decisions about the relationship quickly. Wait a while—at least a few months—to find out if there is a flip side to the behavior. A dear friend of mine who was married to someone like this would actually recommend that you give the relationship a couple of years before you commit to it. For some people—and this could depend on a stage of life, medication, and a lot of other factors—the swing in the other direction may not occur quickly.

Can you deal with one man who is two different people?

PSYCHOPATHS
Guys Who Always Make *You* the Loser

Every now and then you meet someone who has it all. Good looks, good conversation, and he has done everything—at least everything interesting. You know the type. Backpacked through Europe and spoke to people he encountered in the native languages. Cares about his fellow man. Answers every question intelligently, or at least humorously. Emotionally intense from the beginning. Act as though he's known you all of your life . . . and maybe in a past life as well. You feel as though you know him through and through: He engenders absolute trust. How should you feel? Sick to your stomach.

This would describe a profile I have referred to my entire professional life as "glossy." He's so shiny that nothing sticks to him. With a source like this, I perceive that he is reading me and feeding me what I want to hear. The result is a natural tendency to trust him—which is an unnatural state for me. These glossy people are like a shellacked photo: If you spill something on it, you can wipe it off. Commonly, these people have learned what they can get away with over a lifetime of doing it. They constantly prod for acceptance and walk the knife's edge of personal risk. They flirt with danger, and they flirt with you as though they have nothing to lose. If you call them on the bluff, you are simply a stupid bitch in their eyes.

How to Spot One

In *Without Conscience,* Robert D Hare, Ph.D., discusses the traits of a psychopath. Dr. Hare created the "Psychopathy Checklist," which, in his words, is "a complex clinical tool for professional use." In other words, he does not want this used by amateurs for barroom diagnoses. At the same time, in the words of Oprah, "If it walks like a duck . . ."

What follows is a general summary of the key traits and behaviors of psychopaths as defined by Dr. Hare. If you see this complex collection of behaviors in a guy, steer clear. Take one from me: If I see a dog foaming at the mouth, I do not wait for a clinical test to stay the hell away.

Emotional and interpersonal symptoms for the psychopath are the following:

- Glib and superficial
- Egocentric and grandiose
- Lacking in remorse or guilt
- Lacking in empathy
- Deceitful and manipulative
- Shallow emotionally

Except for "lacking in empathy," this group sounds like professional interrogators. No matter. Dr. Hare says the psychopath can fake that one quite well. The interrogator will often never see the source again, so anything he says means nothing. The interrogator can be glib and superficial about his behaviors, and he may admit things to the source he has never done and would never admit if he had. Because an interrogation is an encounter in which he has absolute control, the interrogator can feel free to be grandiose. He may even point to how important he is in the world and what he can do for you. The interrogator need feel no remorse or guilt because he is justified in what he is doing. (How do you know your interrogator is lying to you? His lips are moving.) We know he is using approaches, so he is deceitful and manipulative. Interrogators learn to compartmentalize their emotions to prevent becoming too attached to the source. The result is shallow emotions shown toward the source.

Dr. Hare writes, "Psychopaths seem to suffer a kind of emotional poverty that limits the range and depth of their feelings. While at times they appear cold and unemotional, they are prone to dramatic, shallow, and short-lived displays of feeling. Careful observers are left with the impression that they are play-acting and that little is going on below the surface." In professing love for you—an emotion that psychopaths cannot experience, according to Hare—these are the guys who might recite poetry because their own words would not authentically capture the emotion of love.

The reason I bring this up is simple: The interrogator is trained to ply these same skills for a cause: that is, the betterment of society. The psychopath has these skills whether simply as a matter of biology or a matter of biology and nurture. Dr. Hare by no means says all psychopaths are the Ted Bundy serial-killer type, *but all serial killers are psychopaths.* Contact with one of these hyper-polished, glossy types typically results in catastrophe.

You and the Psychopath

How do you know on first meeting whether or not you might be faced with a psychopath? The chances are not as small as you might think. If Dr. Hare is correct, roughly three million people in the United States alone qualify as psychopaths.

Is your man too intense? You might counter by saying that "too" is relative. The question is, "Is he too intense *for you*?" Does the fact that he wants to crawl inside your psyche within five minutes of meeting you make you even a little uncomfortable?

Is he putting on airs?

There are instances when someone is genuine and the two of you just click. It's fireworks, as the dating commercials say. Napalm is fireworks, too. Give this newfound soul mate a little time to prove he is a soul mate and not just good at exploiting weakness. I am not saying keep your distance, but do keep your eyes open.

If you see him again, dig for telling facts. Find out if he rides that bike on his car roof. Make sure that puppy he walks in front of your apartment doesn't live in a crate the other twenty-three hours a day. If you insist on answers to the questions about the intriguing and alluring aspects of him, you will have a good shot at weeding out not only the psychopaths but also the "harmless" phonies.

In this process of exploring whether a guy has real value, is nothing but a collection of tricks, or is actually dangerous, you will need to remember some genuinely good guys do not know how to break the ice. They come across badly and sometimes strangely. But you have every right to ask the hard questions so you can be sure.

Love or Captivity

In simulating wartime capture situations at SERE school, we throw a hood over the "prisoner's" head and bind his arms and legs with a cord in the middle of the night. And while he's still disoriented, we begin the interrogation.

When the man you're with suddenly abuses you, why don't you rebel and run out the door? The shock of capture robs you of your ability to make rational choices. Your mind has no file drawer to store the data coming in about this overpowering new experience.

You wouldn't be reading this book if you wanted to get into a relationship that failed and made you miserable. You step through the D.E.C.O.D.E. process and do your best to find the right guy, but you may still end up with a psychopath, a narcissist, or somebody with mood swings that may or may not stem from mental illness. Why? As I said earlier in this chapter, these men can be so skilled at disguising the symptoms of their abnormalities that they can sometimes even fool professionals.

When you do realize that your life has taken a sharp turn into gloomy territory, you desperately search for reasons why this incident is not a sign of failure. It's just a misunderstanding. A problem that can be fixed tomorrow.

As you make excuses and try to cope, you might wake up one day and realize your man has trapped you—cut you off from family and friends and *required* certain behavior changes "or else." Now, you have been not only captured like a prisoner of war but confined as well. The persistent feeling of walking on eggshells dominates this scenario. Day to day, the required-or-else behavior may change, so your life becomes a series of displaced expectations. This helps him establish the role of being perfect.

Interrogators are professional anxiety brokers; the only difference between them and abusive partners is the word "professional." The techniques of both are the same: Set up unrealistic expectations and then alternately reward and punish so the person cannot know what to expect next and is constantly on edge. He routinely violates entitlements in the relationship as part of the manipulation. You have the right to expect gratitude after serving a great dinner; sometimes he gives it, and sometimes he mocks the dinner and the cook. You have a right to honesty, respect for your relationship with your God, confidence that your partner won't take your personal possessions, and a number of other basic entitlements. Everyone has those rights in a love relationship.

The players in an interrogation relationship do not have those rights, however. That is why the abused and abuser have so much in common with the wartime prisoner and the captor. For any abused woman, just like a captive, the consuming concern is self-preservation, so she's constantly asking herself, "Am I doing the right thing or the wrong thing?" Just as in the prisoner-of-war relationship, only the captor can answer the question. Out of all of the tools I've given you to find the right guy, rely the most on the lessons regarding entitlement.

Ask yourself, and do it every day if you have any suspicions that you're headed in a dangerous direction, "Do we have a clear, stated understanding of which entitlement violations are deal-breakers?" Is your man open to discussing a misunderstanding about expectations, rather than flying into a rage as a default response? Or does he appear to shut down emotionally and respond with bone-chilling meanness?

I want to give you a little more insight into what could happen if you fail to ask the tough questions about entitlements. One scenario ends in physical abuse. The guy slaps you around, beats you, or maybe even pushes you out of bed—anything to make you physically uncomfortable. You are forced into limbic mode, which is the state in which your emotions take over and block your ability to think. A part of your brain called the amygdala goes into overdrive. Here's where you might say you reach the point of no return. *Psychoeducation.org* describes the situation like this:

The amygdala seems to respond to severe traumas with an unstable fear response. That sustained state of fear will erode your health, your appearance, and your mind. You could literally end up stumbling through life in a confusion over what to do next—is it right or wrong? Is it caring or cruel?

Another scenario ends in mental and emotional abuse, without any physical mistreatment. Your scars are from hearing, "You idiot. You moron. You fail to meet my standards." After a while, and it doesn't necessarily take long, depending on the fragility of your psyche to begin with, you look in the mirror and see a woman who has no value.

Whether it's actual torture or psychological torture, the resulting feeling that you're worthless makes you less able to resist his pressure. You are officially a victim; that's how you adapt. His tactics systematically remove your identity so you feel you have to give him sole and absolute power to dictate how and when you will accommodate him.

As a result, you're not in a position to rescue yourself, and you cannot assume your family or friends will rescue you, either. Guys who do this invariably separate you from family and friends. They are blocked from learning about your hideous situation firsthand, and you don't even have the ability to seek their input. At that point, just like any sequestered prisoner, you start to think that your perverted world is normal. Even when it gets worse, you won't necessarily notice it. Ever heard that myth about the frogs? Put a frog in a pot of hot water, and it will jump out. Put it in cold water and turn up the temperature, and it will not notice the change and boil to death. (This isn't true, by the way, but the lesson is valid.)

How does a woman get to be a victim in the first place? Go back to the early exercises about the voices in your head, how much your opinions reflect the thinking of others, and how you see yourself.

Let's say that the woman now being held hostage by a lunatic lover began life as a model child and superior student for whom success seemed inevitable. She fell in love with a handsome lawyer and they moved in together. Shortly after that, her life consisted of a steady diet of relentless criticism of clothes, cooking, and cellulite. Taking a positive, productive approach, she kept thinking that he only said those things to help her, to improve her looks and her skills. Otherwise, why would be bother? The days became weeks and the weeks became years. In a nutshell, that's how it happens.

What I've observed with prisoners is that there's a little box inside everyone's head that contains pride of accomplishment/fear of failure. When you find out how to reach it, you can manipulate the contents. As an interrogator, I would do simple things centered on a source's fear of failure to manipulate him. I would put two food tins in front of him and say, "Pick one." He picks one, and it's empty. "Oh, well. Guess you don't eat today." Of course, both tins were empty. Because it's illegal to withhold food, the prisoner would get dinner anyway, but I still proved to him that he was a failure by giving him dinner out of pity. Time after time, I would do things like this to convince a prisoner, "You're always wrong. I'm always right."

A critical element of the success of this tactic is that people need interaction with other human beings, and that need can be met by the creepiest human being. If the only steady contact you have is with a man eroding your self-esteem, your need is being met in a sick way that will eat away at your very core. You feel the only way to achieve self-worth is through compliance; this is commonly known as the Stockholm syndrome, that is, the sense of relationship that a captive feels for the captor. The captor convinces the person that the only way to feel worthwhile again is to see his point of view and acquiesce.

Are there times when a man will do this subconsciously, rather than with premeditation? Sure, but the result is the same for the victim. The worst thing she can do is say, "He doesn't mean it," or "It's not his fault." A wild tiger doesn't mean to hurt your feelings by ripping into your throat.

In some cases, probably rare due to the fear factor, a woman will have an affair to escape. She finds a man who seems to respect entitlements and, particularly, seems to know how to honor what's in her little pride-of-accomplishments box. He's nothing more than the "good cop" in an interrogation, the one who gets your trust for no other reason than he isn't mean to you. It's a bad start to a relationship, and an unproductive escape route.

So how do you escape? Here's what you do, or what you tell a friend to do if you suspect that she's being sucked into this kind of captor-captive relationship:

- External input is essential. Get help because your judgment can no longer be trusted.

- Use the following techniques to help you restore some cognitive thought. These are efforts to change the ground rules about arguing, criticism, and even small talk. I want to emphasize that these are tactics I refined as an interrogator; I leave the therapy to the therapists.
  - Only argue about things you know about. Do not try to wing it; stick with the facts.
  - Don't get defensive. When he criticizes you, avoid the "but" speeches: "But you've gained weight, too." Instead, say nothing or go for the solution: "Want to go for a walk after dinner?"
  - Derail a discussion that's heating up. He criticizes your driving (again), so you start talking about an antique car you saw downtown today. Be prepared for him to tell you that you can't follow a logical train of thought if you do this, even though it may be successful in the short-term as an argument deterrent. If he does, let his criticism serve as a reminder that you should get help and get out.

12.

Emphasize the Good

As an interrogator, I reinforce positive behavior by giving a prisoner something in exchange for some concession on his part. I relieve the pressure on him physically or psychologically. It might be an act as simple as not yelling or standing a little farther away to give him a sense of personal space whenever he does what I ask. On the other hand, if he's uncooperative, I ratchet up the pressure until he capitulates. It's pressure-release, pressure-release, and it works well on most people. In fact, we all get it—at work, in relationships, from teachers. When I do this in the interrogation room, the source feels as though it is normal behavior, that is, something to be expected.

Getting subtle enough for that kind of push-pull to be effective takes practice, even in the interrogation room. Real life is a different story. You cannot constantly manipulate, nor is that what this "emphasize" process is all about. This process is about rewarding behavior you want and discouraging behavior you don't. Your outcomes are built on process steps.

Steps to the Outcome You Want

Those steps need to include the behaviors you are willing to accept *long-term,* or the outcome is likely to be a stew of things you do not want. So, even if long-term means three months for you, evaluate what behaviors you want to see three months from now. Do not make the dating version of the I-want-that-choco-late-lab-because-he-is-cute-never-mind-my-400-square-foot-studio mistake.

You've probably seen at least one of the many movies about the trials of being a stepparent. Typically, the kids won't do chores, or they won't do them to the stepmom's standards. At some point, she figures out that unless she finds an engaging way to reward good behavior and take inflexible disciplinary measures when the kids don't do the chores, she will not make any progress.

In short, you need to find the *best* way to emphasize the things you want this guy to do and to offer no reinforcement for the negative. If you always take a negative approach—"do this or you can just forget about sex!"—then the word to describe you is *bitch.* Negative reinforcement may seem to work in the short run, but it won't work in the long term. That's the "The beatings will continue until morale increases" concept.

If you always take a positive approach, no one will call you a bitch, but you have to be careful how to do it or you may not get exactly what you want, either. The operative word is balance.

There are lots of ways to win. Here's an example of contrasts. You and your man go out to dinner with three of your girlfriends. He likes one of them, marginally enjoys the company of another, and strongly dislikes the third. He makes obvious and rude noises about wanting to go home before the dessert menu arrives. Ways to handle this include the following:

- Leaving precisely when he complains.
   MEANING You reward bad behavior with positive outcome.
   ➡ **RESULT** You are guaranteed to get this behavior again; in short, he does what he wants and gets what he wants.
- Suggest to him in a side conversation that he'd better be nice or he will sleep alone for a while.
   MEANING Your default is to "mom" him by throwing around an "or else" whenever he misbehaves.
   ➡ **RESULT A** He will obey—at least this time.
   ➡ **RESULT B** He will comply, but he will also resent your power play. That could lead to an argument or even a breakup.
   ➡ **RESULT C** His resentment is so strong that he makes your life a living hell by instigating issues so that your friends never want him—and maybe you—around again.
- Stay through the end of dinner and make it clear afterward that he will always have the ability to opt out of such a get-togethers in the future.
   MEANING You offer a reasonable and positive out in a manner that is respectful to all concerned.
   ➡ **RESULTS** He feels as though you're doing him a favor. He feels more positive toward you in the long run, and you still get to spend time with your friends. And the big payoff is that you set expectations for when the really big conflicts come along.

Again, the "emphasize" process is not about manipulation—making him do something different. It is about rewarding good behavior and not rewarding bad behavior. In summary, you will stay sensitive to his rituals, noticing if anything changes when you do something, while you use approaches to maintain the good behavior and marginalize or eliminate those you hate.

While you go through this final "E" part of D.E.C.O.D.E., remember Woman Mistake Number One: You cannot change a man. *Your power lies in your ability to motivate him to want to change himself.* There are some basic considerations to this process.

Be Consistent with Entitlements

Through discussions and simply paying attention, get a firm grasp of the entitlements relevant to your relationship; see where the lines are so you don't cross them carelessly. If you understand this part of your relationship, you will naturally go about emphasizing positive outcomes, rather than trying to manipulate him into becoming who you want.

I shouldn't have to tell you, for instance, that I would dump you quickly if you asked me to get rid of my horses. One look at my lifestyle should be all you need to know that I have profound entitlements related to my horses. To put it bluntly, no woman is coming between me and my horses. So if you're in an analogous situation with a man who loves dogs, or race cars, or poker, it's your problem if you want him to drop that, not his. Go back to the beginning of this book and realize that you should not be in the process of trying to transform this guy's priorities; instead, you should re-examine what you want in a man.

You will accomplish nothing by inadvertently violating many kinds of entitlements in the interest of "positive reinforcement." A friend who loves surprises for birthdays, Christmas, Valentine's Day, and you-name-it day thought that she would throw her boyfriend a surprise birthday party to reinforce the message. His sense of privacy and desire for control overrode any enjoyment he experienced at seeing thirty friends show up unexpectedly. Instead of celebration and more surprises, the experience led to an argument and then to a truly imbalanced compromise that cannot last in the long term: no surprises.

Identify Personality Types

Consider the personality type you're dealing with, as well as the type you are, in how you conduct this reinforcing exercise. If you are focused on "Don't do that," rather than on "Do that," your actions will have a different character.

As a default-negative personality, when I teach people how to ride horses, I focus on what they are doing wrong so I can solve the problem. Some people can't take that and they complain, "You always tell me what I messed up and never tell me what I did right!" I say to them, "You tell me what you're doing right. I tell you what you're doing wrong so that I can help you change those things." The right things are already there, so I don't feel a need to address them. That alienates some people, so I have to change my approach to get the desired result.

You not only need to classify yourself as someone who defaults to a positive judgment or defaults to a negative one, you also have to classify him. Will a negative action on your part, even one aimed squarely at producing a solution to a problem, arouse resentment and cause him to shut down?

Honor the Role of Rituals

Take your relationship and personal rituals into consideration in two ways—during and after the ritualistic events.

Tread carefully on rituals related to the big primal urges—sex, food, and sleep. Disrupting them is bound to create fights and outcomes that you will not like. Let's say you know he has a trip wire, that is, a point of no return, in an argument. When you sense he is nearing it, back away before you immerse yourself in damaging issues. And if you have developed relationship rituals, such as going to bed at ten or eating dinner at seven, look for deviations in these to indicate the health of the relationship. Lots of behavior-modification work to get him to come to bed on time is not worth anything if he no longer wants to sleep with you.

New rituals come out of positive change. Watch for them.

Using Effective Approaches

To figure out the most effective approach, go back to the discussion of the seven deadly sins and look at the positive indicators that describe his behavior. If his behavior falls on the good side of greed, then the incentive approach will likely be the best. If it's pride, use pride-and-ego (up).

Keep in mind that if it is pride, for example, then he may be extremely controlling as a result of that pride. So, whatever action you decide to take in reinforcing good behavior, make sure it does not undermine his sense of control. For example, let's say you want him to have a monthly "big date night," when both of you get dressed up. Sort of like a grown-up prom night. In your mind, that will serve as an important reminder that you are special to each other. He agrees, but you always pre-empt him in making the reservations. Bad move.

Most things you want out of someone are going to come in increments. They won't happen overnight. If you want him to open the door for you and carry your bags, and he was not raised to do that, but you see he's willing to grow in that direction, you will need to repeat the reinforcement to produce change in stages that build on each other.

Sometimes eliciting positive outcomes will mean adapting yourself. You may be physically strong enough to carry a fifty-pound bag of potting soil, but if you enjoy having the help and respectful attention of a guy, don't be arrogant about carrying it. Go to the gym and lift a fifty-pound dumbbell instead of discouraging his well-intended action.

Don't fool yourself about outcomes. You can take a series of actions and get what you want for now, but it may not be what you want in a long-term relationship. For example, you could set yourself for a dating relationship involving casual sex in exchange for lots of behaviors you like, but do you want them for the next ten years?

I am not teaching you magic so you can change basic personality traits. If there's any magic in this, it's a process that helps you clearly establish what is significant, and nonnegotiable, to each of you. That is your foundation for a respectful relationship that clarifies what is tolerable, allowable, and desirable. Remember the pyramid ranking entitlements. If you try to change the peak of the pyramid, he will dump you. If he tries to change the peak of yours, you *should* dump him.

This "emphasize" part of D.E.C.O.D.E. is aimed as much at you as it is at him. Too many women strengthen behaviors that they do not like by thinking it is sexy in the beginning, with no concept of the outcome of reinforcing that behavior. If you repeatedly support those behaviors—sexual, monetary, hygiene, respect, or any others that offend you—you will get what you deserve. In retail terms: You break it; you bought it.

Conclusion

I can establish my information collection criteria, use all of my interrogator tricks and tools, come up with the right guy, and suddenly find that a different prisoner meets my needs better. Or I might find that my information requirements have changed. For either reason, I stop investing my time in the first prisoner and turn my full attention to the second. That may actually hurt the first guy's feelings because I've built a rapport with him. I've also reinforced particular expectations through approaches like "incentive" and "pride-and-ego (up)," as described in Chapter 7. My original source got used to certain concessions and compliments and now all of that will go away.

Dating is all about finding the best guy to meet your needs, and your needs can change. You have to keep using the D.E.C.O.D.E. tools at various stages of the relationship. As much as you feel connected to the guy whose phone number you just programmed into your cell phone, he may be history before you get a new phone.

In the process of going through this book, you may have discovered what your real requirements are. Or they may have evolved as you began to use the interrogation tools to evaluate and observe a broader spectrum of individuals. Another possibility is that your first go-round with the tools may have been very mechanical, but once you got used to using them, your experiences returned different information to you about the same guy.

As an interrogator, I need to know who I am and where my vulnerabilities lie at every stage of the dance. I need to know what I am looking for when I go into the interrogation room. I sort through the masses to find just the right one. When I target him, I learn as much as I can before starting to get into conversation. The most dangerous thing I can do is project my needs onto the prisoner to make him the solution.

We do this in the dating world all the time and much to our detriment. As a young man, I dated women whom I "knew" were it . . . until I scratched the surface. And I can only imagine what they thought of me after looking under the hood. We all look for soul mates as if there was someone who could complete who we are. Even if that person exists and you do not know who you are, how would you find him? You have options. Stumble through life blindly hoping for the right person to come along, or proceed as you do in the rest of your life: Develop a skill set to help you do it right. This is the skill set you need.

INDEX

About the Authors

GREG HARTLEY and MARYANN KARINCH are the coauthors of *How to Spot a Liar*. Hartley graduated from the U.S. Army Interrogation School, the Anti-Terrorism Instructor Qualification Course, the Principle Protection Instructor Qualification Course, several Behavioral Symptom Analysis Seminars, and SERE (Survival, Evasion, Resistance, Escape) school. He lives in Atlanta. Karinch is the author of nine books, most of which are about aspects of human behavior. She is an accomplished extreme athlete and holds a master's degree in theatre from The Catholic University of America. She lives in Estes Park, CO.